Dalit Women

in Indian Patriarchal Society

Dalit Women
in Indian Patriarchal Society

Suraiya Shahin

AUTHORSPRESS

Worldwide Circulation through Authorspress Global Network
First Published in 2022
by
Authorspress
Q-2A Hauz Khas Enclave, New Delhi-110 016 (India)
Phone: (0) 9818049852
E-mail: authorspressgroup@gmail.com
Website: www.authorspressbooks.com

Dalit Women in Indian Patriarchal Society
ISBN 978-93-5529-158-5

Printed in India by Manipal Technologies Limited, Manipal

I dedicate this book to
my dear daughter Naira Arsheen

Acknowledgements

I am indebted to my parents who have always been performing as great guides to me by giving me good opportunities in making my career. Their encouragement always boosted me up to do better performances in my life. Without their co-operation, I would not be able to write this book today.

I thank my loving husband who performs as the best life partner for me. He is the person who understands and reads my passionate mind. He has always been encouraging me to write books. Without his co-operation, this book would not have been completed. I also thank him for reading this book on its completion and commenting on it.

I also thank professor as well as Nigerian prolific writer, Bukar Usman, who appeared as a great inspirer to me. My thanks also go to the Nigerian prolific writer, Ifeoma Okoye who kept inspiring me to be creative in the literary field.

I am indebted to the libraries of many universities such as Sahitya Academy, New Delhi, Jawaharlal Nehru, and others from where I accessed the relevant materials to study. My special thanks go to Jamia Millia Islamia University, New Delhi, India, where I completed my M.Phil and also got the good opportunity to do my Ph.D. This university provided me lots of relevant materials and a cozy environment to be a creative soul. It also gave me a competitive platform to read more and more extra things apart from the course works and my book is the outcome of such a highly competitive platform. I thank this university whose library and campus I sat hours and hours to think and write this book.

Suraiya Shahin

Contents

Introduction

> "Turn in any direction you like, caste is the monster that crosses your path. You cannot have political reform; you cannot have economic reform, unless you kill this monster".
>
> B.R. Ambedkar (*The Annihilation of Caste)*

Caste is one of the most important elements of our country, India. In this society, the moment an infant comes out from its mother's womb his/her caste and gender is assigned first. Caste and gender are like a stamp on a baby's body. Caste and gender determine one's particular identity in our country. Almost in most of the families, a baby is brought up on the basis of gender. In the same way, a baby born in a schedule caste family is taken as 'untouchable'. If a baby is born in upper caste family then everything goes well. Leading a free life is far easier in such a family. But on the contrary, life is like a fetter if one is born in a lower caste family.

In India, it's very problematic to get a full-free life for lower caste people especially women. At every step, they have to face their imposed caste discrimination, tortures, and public humiliations. Caste invariably determines their worth, their mind, their ideas or thoughts, and their standard of living in the public's eyes. Caste, in our Indian society is rooted in such a way that everything, every work is measured on the basis of caste. The caste system is inevitably in its glaring form here in our country. Before eating or drinking in other's house, people first of all try to know the caste of that person lest be polluted with the Untouchables. A man can't touch the next one simply because he belongs to a lower caste. In every field, caste system is prevalent even today. There is a difference in caste and class system. Class system refers to the economic disparities while the caste system refers to certain caste belief. Class system does not bring any untouchability as the caste system is a curse for Untouchables. Class disparity will automatically come to end as soon caste disparity is rooted out from our society. Likewise casteism, gender has been a curse for our Indian society. On the one side our Hindu religious books portray women in some glorified incarnation but on the other side, men don't spare the moments to subjugate women. A woman's identity is determined by her individual gender.

This book is all about the social crises that tend to marginalise dalit women on the basis of caste. It captures the prevailing discriminatory nature of a particular society by throwing light on certain threads of patriarchy that have been crippling in Dalit women's development.

Suraiya Shahin

CHAPTER 1

Formation of Patriarchy

The term patriarchy is a universally acknowledged term. More or less no family, no private or public place is free from such a persistence concept. Patriarchy is nothing but a persistent social structure and a weapon to control, constrain, exploit and oppress women. It occurs in every day conversation. The question here arises that from where does the term 'patriarchy' emerge?

If defining patriarchy in general term, it is applied for the rule and authority of man over the entire family including women. Patriarchy does not refer domination of males only over women but it also encompasses the domination over younger males of the family. In a patriarchal family a "man" is usually taken as the owner or head of the family. But the process as well as the nature of patriarchy invariably differs from culture to culture, religion to religion, caste to caste, and class to class. The ways of women's subjugation are not alike in every culture or every caste. If we see in the context of India we find Brahminical patriarchy, Dalit patriarchy, Muslim Patriarchy, and tribal patriarchy. The subordination of women in developed countries like America and England is very much different from the developed countries like India, Pakistan, Nigeria, and others. Men, since time immemorial, have been figures of the authority having control over women, both in the domestic as well as the public sphere. India has been traditionally a society where social, political, economic and family-control remain in the hands of men who formulate norms, thereby excluding women from any form of public participation.

On the other side, the term 'matriarchy' refers to the social structure where a woman actively rules over the family or possesses decisive power. But matriarchy hardly exists in our country like India. Matriarchy had been widely in practice in the southern parts of India like Kerala where a woman was regarded superior in the family. Women run the family. But now matrilineal power is also getting change even at those places. Patriarchy is now substituting matriarchy there. To some extent, we can see matrilineal power currently in process among the Khasi people, who live in Meghalaya and Assam. In Assam even today there are many families where the property is passed through females. Household or any ritual is autonomous for women. In such families, there is no resentment from the side of men but on the top of it, men are very much interested in participating equally in all the celebrations.

Origin of the Term "patriarchy"

The word "patriarchy" originates from the Greek word *patriarkhia* which refers to masculine dominance over the family. According to Gerda Lerner, "the dominance of male members as the head of the family over their kin is much older than classical antiquity; it begins in the third millennium B.C. and is well established at the time of the writing of the Hebrew Bible" (239). It is a historic creation institutionalised by ancient people as a social structure that took about 2500 years to its completion.

Engels, the Marxist theorist is of the view that the system of patriarchy is not rooted since the evolution of human beings but it developed with the development of wealth and capitalism. Human societies in ancient times were egalitarian, and a type of solidarity occurred between men and women. Of course, there was a division of labour between men and women but it was a simple division of outside and inside works. The main jobs of men was to work outside regarding hunting, fishing, and acquiring raw materials for food while women handled home caring children, preparing food, and washing clothes. Human beings were nomadic, so they kept wandering from place to place in search of food and shelter. But as soon as they settled at one place, things changed and the mind of the people changed towards development, and their attention shifted towards accumulating wealth. When human beings began to cultivate crops, they began animal husbandry. As the production of goods accelerated, the communist nature of society got changed gradually. Conflicts arose over the control of resources. In this way, there was a division of labour into two classes: master and slaves, the exploiters and the exploited. Gradually as people started accumulating wealth, it brought a change in the relationship between men and women. When men began to produce more and more wealth they wished to keep all wealth safe only for themselves. Earlier men also used to contribute to domestic works but as soon as production increased, domestic work lost its importance, and it became a private domain of women. Men started giving more values to outside production rather than private works of home, the household works were being started to be considered 'a private service': the wife became the first domestic servant. She was rather deprived of public social production. Domestic works were expropriated by men and devalued which led women in becoming domestic slaves. Then the emergence of private property encompassed land, animals, or slaves and later it came to include women as well. Men wanted to own women so that they could continue control over the children, and they needed to do it only to pass on their wealth to the next generation. Earlier mother-right was in dominance rather than father-right. As patriarchal power increased; women lost all rights. In this way, the rule of the father came into existence, and the system of patriarchy came into existence. (Engels 73-155)

Gerda Lerner also makes her points about the mobilisation of patriarchy with the development of agriculture and more and more production. Men as sole producers of agriculture and hunting had started to control women but women contradictorily were deprived of the same right. Women were exchanged in marriage for the benefit of their families. And later they were conquered in slavery where they became sexual objects of the victorious people. While the other theorist, Hartmann, asserts that the norms of patriarchy predate capitalism and hence the exploitation of women is not new through capitalist society. She goes on to say that both housework and wage labour are important sites of women's thread of subjugation by men. The outside field jobs are valued more than house works. Men themselves organise to divide the respective works marginalising women thus women's disadvantaged position in paid work makes them more vulnerable. Men never admit the fact that women within the home do more labour than men but they are left unpaid. Their jobs within the home are not taken seriously. Einstein, the theorist, views patriarchy assigns a system of control and law and order, while capitalism operates a social structure of the economy.

It would be wrong if we take a single thread operating to patriarchy. There are multiple ways through which patriarchy operates into a further continuous process. We can see the patriarchal operation first by husband; patriarchal weapon associated with waged labour; male violence on the road; patriarchal relation through gender and sexuality. Each and every thread of patriarchy is closely associated with the assigned social established codes. They embody overall prevailed constellation of social relations which structure gender disparities.

There are two main types of patriarchy: external and internal patriarchy. Internal patriarchy operates inside the four walls of a home where women's words are not valued or taken lightly. Male members of the family take complete hold of the family. While external patriarchy takes place outside the home. External patriarchy does not exclude women from the public arena but rather subordinates them through all the ways. It is the external patriarchal modes through which women are harassed at the official place and pushed to be socially vulnerable. Male generally create violence in the form of power over all women. It occurs on regular basis. It is seen in various forms including rape, wife-beating, sexual harassment at work, flashing, using abusive language for women accordingly her body shape.

Mythical Concept of Patriarchy

A woman's secondary status is largely associated with Biblical mythical concepts. It is regarded as the origin of patriarchal period during the first half of the second millennium B.C. of biblical history. The book of Genesis has presented women in a subordinate position to that of men. The Biblical story of James Version contends that God created Adam first and later Eve was created out of Adam's rib. "And the man said: 'This is now bone of my bone and flesh; she shall be called Woman because she was taken out of man'" (Genesis 3: 23). The creation of Woman out of Man's hands signifies the imposition of Man as a creator of woman – woman was created as a part of man hence Man must embrace her. And they shall be one flesh. Man's giving birth process to Woman signifies the authorial power like God to humankind. By this act of God's made respective place for man and woman; he has authority over her as part and parcel of his body. This authority implies interconnection and interdependency on each other.

John Calvin comments that Adam was taught to take his wife as a mirror in which a man sees his face; and Eve, in return had to submit herself willingly to her husband. The Woman's emergence out of Adam's rib is taken significantly to interpret God's assigned inferior place of woman. If we have a look on John Calvin's interpretation we find Man-Woman assigned motif behind creation:

> Since in the person of the man the human race had been created, the common dignity of our whole nature was without distinction.... The woman . . . was nothing else than an accession to the man. Certainly, it cannot be denied, that the woman also, though in the second, was created in the image of God. . . We may therefore conclude that the order of the nature implies that the woman should be helper of the man. The vulgar proverb, indeed, is, that she is a necessary evil; but the voice of God is rather to be heard, which declares that woman is given as a companion and an associate to the man, to assist him to live well. (Cited in Lerner 183)

The mythical concept reveals a woman's subordinate position and the concept of patriarchy rooted in Adam and Eve's fall. When Adam and Eve were living in paradise, they were angels and they were unaware of sexual knowledge. God had forbidden them from tasting the tree of knowledge, "Of every tree in the garden thou mayest freely eat; but the tree of the knowledge of good and evil, thou shalt not eat of it; for in the day that thou eatest thereof thou shalt surely die" (Gen 2: 16-17). After tasting the fruit from 'the tree of knowledge of good and evil' they were expelled from paradise and thrown to earth for the procreation of mankind. Then God punished them by dividing work according to their gender. God said to Adam "'Cursed is the ground for thy sake; in sorrow shalt thou eat of it all the days of thy life'. To Eve He said, I will greatly multiply thy sorrow and thy conception; in sorrow thou shalt bring forth children; and thy desire shall be thy husband, and he shall rule over thee" (Genesis 3: 16). From that day woman's sexual pleasure results in pain and suffering by bearing children. Because of Eve's misleading activity women, even today are denied in most of the public participation and their character is marked as corrupted or distrustable for it was Eve (woman) who brought sin into this world. Although Eve is to be honoured as a life giver, bearer of babies, she shall be definitely ruled by her husband. So, in this way such mythical legend dictates the patriarchal role of the man assigned to women. Thus Book of Genesis has represented women's lower position inevitably different from those of men. In Islamic religious book, the *Quran*, there are some similarities of Biblical notions. In *Quran,* there is a description of Adam and Yahwa. And Yahwa is regarded secondary in the relation of Adam. *Quran* to some extent also tells us a woman has to respect her husband and follow her husband's words to the extremity of looking at his likes and dislikes. Hindu religious texts *Gita and Ramayan* also say that a wife has to take her husband in the form of lord and worship the husband by touching his legs.

Brahminical Patriarchy

All the religious books have relegated women to a secondary position. Indian mythological texts implicitly have glorified women through the examples of Savitri, Sita, Damayanti, Nalayini, and many others reflecting their virtues. According to Hindu religious books, all women are subordinate to men and are expected to obey their husbands. The Hindu religious book *Mahabharata* (XIII. 38.30) points out, "Women have been sinful from the very beginning when the creator first made the five gross elements, and he gave shape to men and women". The *Mahabharata* text itself has been manufactured on a very strong patriarchal imagination. It was a clash between Brahmins and minorities. Vaisyas consisted of a group of minorities. There were one hundred Kauravas while Pandavas were only with a few numbers of five. The hundred Kauravas who represented a group of Dalit community fought against determinately the Brahminical religion. They were fighting for land and kingdom. Even the other Hindu religious book *Ramayana* regards most women as essentially weak and sinful. Agastya, the sage in the *Ramayana* (III.13.5) utters that it has been women's nature ever since creation began to be with a man happily only when he prospers and desert him when he suffers hard days. He takes women as of fickle nature who keep changing as the time changes.

The *Ramayana* reveals how Brahmanism remained successful in establishing all types of patriarchies. The matter here draws our attention to know why Kama and Krishna embody two different values. It is a widely known fact that Kama was born of a Kshatriya woman Kunti, who belonged to a Dalit family. So, he grew up in a dalit family. While Krishna was brought up by Yadavas followed Kshatriya ethnicities. During the war, Kama represented the majority while Krishna represented the minority. But ultimately Kama was killed in the trapping of the fight through conspiracy. The majority of people were adamant about not giving land to them which they had gained through labouring hard. Ultimately, Krishna not getting any alternate to own it created violence. While some of his members of the group (like Arjuna) were reluctant to join such a lethal violence. Krishna pressurised him to indulge in the violent elements to defeat the minorities as the opposite parties were rebelling against brahmins. Eventually, the Brahmins defeated the minorities for the sake of gaining land. It is the same as what we see in *Gita*, the elements and nerves of violence, karma, and varna dharma. *Gita* emerged as a sacred strong text in the context of Brahmins' victory. Through this religious Brahminical book it was ensured to people that whatever is in *Gita* is the victory of Brahmins and defeat of minorities. But it's fact that even this religious book distorts history. It doesn't tell us the reality of the essence of minorities' defeat but it simply portrays the defeat of minorities hiding the truth of why they lost the battle.

During the fight in our country for Country-independence Mahatma Gandhi who belonged to Baniya community strongly propagated the message of *Gita* to reinforce Brahminical hegemony. Gandhi was also containing some particular conspiracy behind his mask of spreading the *Gita* message.

Simultaneously, Dr. Ambedkar could understand minutely the political conspired elements of Mahatma Gandhi. Perceiving the political motifs of brahmins Dr. Ambedkar led to a critique against the established manipulation of brahmins. He has strongly castigated Krishna's brutal act, in his *Riddles of Rama and Krishna and of the Gita.* He sketched out well here the conspired role played by Krishna against dalits that assured people the superiority of Brahminical ideology. He was extremely exasperated that both Gandhi's notion and Brahminical ideology were all set to set up Brahminical thoughts as God's prescribed words. Gandhi was also giving a shape of the conservative Hinduism ideology. Brahmanism faith continued after clutch in the system that represented the creation of the image of Krishna in the writing of *Gita.* A vast majority of Indian people agreed on this text words and nobody mustered the courage to interfere against it.

The sketch of Rama and Sita forms the image of man and woman assigned place in Hindu religion. It is said that both Rama and Sita were born in Kshatriya families. Rama is taken as an incarnation of Vishnu. The *Ramayana* text holds in the notion of women's subordination by showing them some mythical examples of religious books. The *Ramayana* states that a wife completely belongs to her husband. She should surrender herself to the feet of her husband. She is subordinate to her husband. The text assigned a patriarchal thread when it said a wife can never be a ruler for her husband including dalit women. The later Brahmins disagreed on the idea of making a relationship between Brahmins and non-Brahmins.

Draupadi and Radha are such figures which refer to the Brahminical mindset. Draupadi is portrayed as a patriarchal figure that had five husbands. Draupadi was a courageous woman who could not let her courage down when she was raped by Senanayak and his army group. She determinately encountered her attackers with her blood-shedding body. Mahasweta Devi, the Bengali female writer and critic is largely exasperated by the social humiliation that the lower caste women are subjected to the cause of untouchability through patriarchal threads. She makes a point, woman's body is a weapon as well as a voice in itself if a woman boldly confronts the terrific situation. She takes the example of an outspoken woman Draupadi whose naked body proved sole possession in the inhumane world. Devi brings forth the epical story of *Mahabharata* while portraying atrocities on Draupadi. Draupadi, the wife of the Pandavas was dragged to the court when her husband lost the game of dice with the Kauravas. She desperately reached at the verge of living-death. She gave a heart-rending cry on the humiliation inflicted upon her before the public. She was seeking protection, honour, and dignity. The place was crowded but she was alone in that crowd; desolated, she, crying, stretching her arms and raising her boiling eyes full of blood uttered, "If you have loved and revered the mothers who bore you and gave you suck, if the honour of wife or sister or daughter has been dear to you, if you believe in God and Dharma, forsake me not in this horror crueler than death!" (*Mahabharata* 93). The sexual attack on Draupadi discloses the Brahminical codes of patriarchal setup prescribed upon women by the law-makers. Nobody came forward to take active action against the sexual violence of Draupadi because she belonged to an untouchable caste. This reflects the hypocritical face of caste ridden-society.

Draupadi's naked body becomes the symbol of revenge. The mutilated and victimised body itself appeared an autonomous voice of flaming protest. Her breasts had been bitten raw, and the nipples torn. Blood was stuck under her arse and around vagina. She was looking at her humiliated body in the moon-lit night. A sense of shame and honour overcame her. She didn't lose her heart and without caring for shame she questioned them strictly, "What more can you do? Can you clothe me? (*Draupadi* 110). When Duchsasana moved his arms to disrobe Draupadi under the instruction of Prince

Duryodhana, she was trembling and imploring him not to do such a heinous crime. As he was unclothing her sari, she implored Divine mercy to show some spiritual power, "O Lord of the World . . . God whom I adore and trust, abandon me not in this dire plight. You are my sole refuge. Protect me. (*Mahabharata* 94). All of a sudden, a spiritual miracle happened where Lord Krishna appeared as her saviour. On one side she was being stripped off but on the other side yards and yards were covering her body through spiritual power.

Radha was also taken into a relationship with Krishna although she was not married to him. After the sketch of Radha as a mythical figure, upper-caste people began to name their distinct daughter Radha but not Draupadi. Its main reason was that she was having five husbands. She was sexually assaulted which is a big shame in the eyes of people. Here it denotes a Hindu patriarchal mind-set that has all respect for a man like Krishna despite his dealing of eight wives but not Draupadi. It refers to the women subjugation and men authorial power where people have much respect for polygamy but they take polyandry mean. This concept reveals the conspiracy to establish patriarchal power during the writing of *Gita.* Hinduism, at that time was gradually institutionalising patriarchal monogamy. Although there was autonomy in the relation of men and women in South India during that time among Dravida dalits but Hinduism showed them a patriarchal path. But even today we see matrilineal dominance in south Asia where people mostly worship Goddess idols more than God idols.

With the *Ramayana,* Hindu Brahmin *rishies* and *munies* brought the figures of Lord Rama, Lakshmana who attacked the tribal oligarchies. Tataki was a renowned dalit woman who was killed by Hindu communities and her state was expropriated by Brahmins. Later the well-known personality Shambuka was also assassinated and his kingdom got usurped immediately. Rama also played treachery with dalit communities. At that time Vali (a tribal king) the ruler of Kishkinda was in light whom Rama never liked as a ruler. Then the Brahmins applied their sharp mind to defeat him. So the Brahmins shook hand with Vali's brother Sugreeva and also with his nephew Anjaneya to spread the net of treachery. And in this way, the Brahmins became successful in killing the famous minority ruler, Vali.

But when the very beautiful dalit woman, Shurpanakha, expressed her desire to marry Rama, he denied pretending that she should better ask Lakshmana. But the dire tragedy occurred when

Lakshmana without delaying a second, cut off her nose and her earlobes on simply opening her tongue before him regarding the intention of marriage with Rama. This tragedy infuriated her brother Ravana who was an ambitious person. In an enraged mood, he kidnapped Sita in revenge. He wanted to teach a big lesson to Rama by kidnapping Sita. It was a fact that Rama had planned to reign over Sri Lanka. So somehow he planned treachery to reach Lanka to kill Ravana. And he remained successful in the treachery of killing Ravana. As soon as Rama killed Ravana the dalit communities of South India were conquered by Brahminical Aryans. Most probably it brought a transitional phase among dalits as they lost Ravana. The killing of Ravana brought a free way for the Brahmin rishies and so they migrated from the North to the whole of South India. In this way, the Brahmins became successful to defeat the dalits and institutionalising the Brahmin authorial patriarchal power over not only south Indian people but whole over India. Later the dalits opposed the power of Brahmins. The evidence of the Bahujan Samaj Party in North India in 1984 shows the opposition of anti-Brahmin political organisation.

It's really disgusting to think that women are portrayed in some menial thoughts in such reputed religious texts. Is it correct what a woman deserves? No, never. Women are represented negatively through religious texts simply because to continue the norms of patriarchy. They are portrayed by giving the examples of religious texts because Indian people have blind faith in religious texts. They take all its words as God-given words. "If we see women's status through the story of *Jataka* (I.155) we find that women were represented in the congenital unstable nature. It says that women can embrace whatever is beside them; that's why they are linked to creeping vines. They are represented as adulterous by nature and insatiable as greedy cows seek pastures anew, they yearn for mate after mate".

The concept of Brahminical patriarchy is rooted in the ancient time and with its mythical concept. Hindu *Brahminical* book *Manusmriti* is all responsible to institutionalise the subjugation of women and supremacy of men. The well-known personality Manu in his text *Manusmriti* has denied the positive aspects of women, and asserts that women are objects who should be always under watch by men, "– in childhood under the father, in wife-hood under the husband and in widowhood under son". There is not a single statement in *Manusmriti* that has denied women's honour or equal position of women but the whole text proves toxic for women especially Dalit women. Manu utters that if a husband wants to keep his offspring pure, he should always guard his wife so that his progeny is not denied to him in the future. And simultaneously he considers women's nature responsible for it that makes men guard them. His menial principles based on complete orthodoxical and patriarchal, to constrain women reflect here in his *Manusmriti*:

- Women do not care for beauty, nor is their attention fixed on age; thinking that it is enough if he is a man, they give themselves to the handsome and the ugly.
- Through their passion for men, through their mutable tempers, through their natural heartlessness they become disloyal towards their husbands, however carefully they may be guarded.
- Women, true to their character, are capable of leading men – a fool and a learned man alike – astray in this world. Both become slaves of desire.
- One should not marry women with reddish hair, redundant body parts (such as six fingers), one who is often sick, one without hair or excessive hair and one with red eyes.
- Wise men should not marry women who do not have a brother and whose parents are not well known in society.
- Prudent men should marry those women who are free from bodily defects, with beautiful names, grace like an elephant, moderate hair on the head and body, soft limbs and small teeth.
- A Brahmin, a true defender of his class, should not have his meals in the company of his wife and should avoid even looking at her. Furthermore, he should not look at her when she is having her meals or when she sneezes/yawns.
- A female child, young woman or old woman is not supposed to work independently even at her place of residence.
- Girls are supposed to be in the custody of their father when they are children, women under the custody of their husband when married, and under the custody of her son as widows. In no circumstances is she allowed to assert herself independently.

- Men may be lacking virtue, be sexual perverts, immoral and devoid of any good qualities, and yet women must not cease to worship or serve their husbands.
- Women have no divine right to perform any religious ritual. Make vows or observe a fast. Her only duty is to obey and please her husband, if she wants to be exalted in heaven.
- In case a lady enjoys sex with a man from a higher caste, the act is not punishable. However, if she enjoys sex with lower caste men, she is to be punished and kept in isolation.
- Brahmin men can marry Brahmin, Kshatriya, Vaishya and even Shudra women but Shudra men can marry only Shudra women. However, in no situation should men from the other castes marry a Shudra woman. If they do so, they would be responsible for the degradation of their family.
- Every man of any caste or even the weak man must have full command over his wife and he should follow it as his strict duty. (Manu 22-42)

These quotes from *Manusmriti* explicitly exhibit that Manu has portrayed women as the weaker sex only to be under the custody of a man. They don't deserve to be freed. Its famous sloka in Sanskrit also states clearly on the freedom of women and merely the object of sex, *"Pita raksahtu komarya, Pati rakshtu yovne, Puta rakshtu vardhakyu, na stri svatratarye arhati"*. Manu has penned down *Manusmriti* to represent women as secondary and oppressed; man as ruler and woman to be ruled. He deceived people into believing that *Manusmriti* is God's words so people have to follow it. He knew that Indian people have blind faith in the religious text so he took the support of this manuscript as a religious book. And he remained successful in deluding people in the institutionalisation of all types of patriarchies.

Such portrayals of women in *Manusmriti* in a negative context provoked Dr. Ambedkar too much and he could not tolerate such heinous thoughts of Manu and opined that the Brahminical texts were largely patriarchal which subsequently compelled him to burn the text *Manusmriti* in 1927, which denied women freedom. Dr. Ambedkar believed in the principle that women should be more and more educated even than men because the process of nurturing completely depends on mothers. A child's mental growth will take its direction if he is brought up properly. Kancha Ilaiah's views on Brahminical patriarchy manifest:

> "Brahminical patriarchy operates on two kinds of mentalities. On the one hand, it creates a mind that can control, manipulate and finally structure: the male mind. On the other hand, it forms a mind that can be manipulated, controlled, and structured: the female mind. It does not provide any scope for questioning, debate and discourse. Its history is a history of recitation of that divine word". (Ilaiah 2002: 44)

Ilaiah interprets that Brahminical women have to survive as sexual objects or as homemakers. Their desire is suppressed into the will of their men as if their existence as well their fate is dependent upon their men. But Dalit patriarchy is loose structured patriarchy and can be tackled more easily than Brahminical patriarchy. Upper caste men regarded themselves as pious and knowledgeable but continued their exploitation of dalit women. The same norms do not apply to their upper-caste women who face the risk of severe punishment if they engage in sexual relations with men belonging to the lower sections of society. It is believed that upper caste women are the paragons of purity who can be ruined by the mere touch of a lower caste man. The rules of Stridharma are enforced only on upper-caste women. On the other hand, marginalised or dalit women are usually excluded from it because of their menial status that makes them prey to men of all classes.

Dalit Patriarchy

Dalit patriarchy is also a perpetuating issue that lies inside Dalits' house where men's dominance takes place largely and women's desire is less valuable. But the investigation reports that internal patriarchy is most common among upper castes in all religions. Upper castes/class women are more victimized through internal patriarchal oppression. But lower caste women hardly tolerate their man's torture. They are not dependent on their man economically. These women sometimes also face internal patriarchal troubles through domestic oppression but they behave tit for tat to revolt against the domestic forces of patriarchy. Dalit women don't digest even the single unfit word of her husband. Even in some Dalit families, women are more dominant than men when they earn more than their male counterparts. Kancha Ilaiah, a Dalit activist does not deny from the system of Dalit patriarchy when he says wife-beating is a pervasive patriarchal practice that is prevalent among all castes. So, Dalit family is no exception to it. In Dalit families, a beaten wife does not tolerate easily such domestic violences. A dalit woman does not hesitate in shouting, abusing, and attacking her husband equally. Sometimes they drag their personal disputes towards the road. There is nothing private in their family. Sometimes their disputes become a public scene.

He further makes his own interpretation that a Brahmin family is completely patriarchal authoritarianism. All the members of a Brahmin family have to follow the dictates of their father. His words become authorial words in the family. But a dalit family is autonomous. There is no as such system where only man alone is lord of the family. We can't deny that dalit family is a patriarchal free family but the patriarchy does exist even amongst dalit but in a different way. In a dalit family, a woman has also the right to hit back against the patriarchal nature of her husband.

After analysing Kancha Ilaiah's views that patriarchy among dalits is 'democratic' Dr. Anita Ghosh decries him delineating in own way saying that dalit women's shouting back and beating back her husband doesn't reflect democratic patriarchy, rather the question here arises why she has to shout if there is no subjugation. Her shriek and shout expose the brutal sexual and economic attack inflicted upon her that she equally resists rendering cries:

> The dalit woman, more often than not is dependent on her own labour. Such labours outside her home from morning till evening. When she comes home, her husband will be waiting to snatch her hard-earned money which is often the only source to feed the family. If she refuses to give him the money, the husband beats her up. The woman shouts back; in this process of resistance, she might beat him back. This is not because of democratic patriarchy in her family. (Prasad 2007: 58-59)

Dr. Anita has correctly asserted that it is nothing but the romanticising impulse towards dalit women that generally dalit writers point out. Dalit male writers invariably idealise dalit women in the archetypical roles of mothers and sisters and try to represent them in audacious roles. It is only to dissemble the double burden that dalit women always carry with them. It is nothing but the internal patriarchy, operating differently, that constrains and subjugates them in an androcentric world.

Of course, patriarchy does exist in Dalit families too but to some extent in a different way. Dalit women are hardly dependent on their men. They equally earn money with their male counterparts. Whatever they earn, try to save it for future needs. But it's disappointing that they are paid less than their male counterparts owing to gender discrimination.

CHAPTER 2

Theorising Feminist Movements

A number of male writers, philosophers, theorists, scientists, and critics until the 1970s considered women to be incapable of creative abilities. However, the latter part of the 19th century witnessed a radical change in the position of women. As a severe resistance, several movements emerged during the 70s, the demand for equality emerged as a new possibility for women's rights. During that time, the term 'ecriture feminine' emerged in France through the writings of Luce Irigaray, Monique Witting, Chantal Chawaf, Julia Kristeva, Catherine Clement, and Helen Cixous which paved way for other women writers across the world. It also enabled them to challenge women's status in a patriarchal society. Luce Irigaray, Julia Kristeva, and Monique Witting have challenged phallogocentrism and contended that men consider themselves, "I am the unified, self-controlled centre of the universe. The rest of the world, which I define as the 'other', has meaning only in relation to man/father, possessor of the phallus" (Showalter 1985: 362). In a way, it indicates that man's central position is reinforced not only by philosophy and religion but also by language that enables them to dominate the world through the use of authorial power.

It was Helen Cixous who first came up with her concept 'ecriture feminism' in her outstanding work *The Laugh of the Medusa* (1975), challenging the phallocentric system of language, advocating that a woman must represent herself in writing, she must write about women and try to fetch women to writing from which they have been deprived violently . She also asserts that women's sexual and intellectual pleasure have been repressed and denied expression which she refers to as 'jouissance'. She attacks men when she harshly utters, "Man is always superior, a victor and a woman passive. Either a woman is passive or she does not exist" (cited in Moi1988: 104). According to Cixous, women's writings alone would be able to subvert the double standards of patriarchal authority that deny a voice to women. Cixous defines how and why women's writing is genderised. She is extremely appalled to see men's minds set-up that underestimates women's writing. Cixous further writes:

> It is impossible to define a feminine practice of writing, and this is an impossibility that will remain, for this practice will never be theorised, enclosed, encoded---which does not mean that it doesn't exist.
>
> Helen Cixous, *The Laugh of Medusa.*

Cixous in her text *The Laugh of Medusa* (1975) admires women's sexuality that is remarkably constant and she even regards it superior to the phallic single-mindedness, as she here explains:

> Though masculine sexuality gravitates around the penis, engendering that centralised body (in political anatomy) under the dictatorship of its parts, woman does not bring about the same regionalisation which serves the couple head/genitals and which is inscribed only within boundaries. Her libido is cosmic, just as her unconscious is world-wide. (Showalter 365)

Women's subjugation over the centuries brought a strong revolution among feminists to resist the dominance of men. So, a group of feminist writers led several feminist movements through waves of feminism to define patriarchy in their own way. The term 'feminist' and 'feminism' emerged from France and developed towards England around in 1894 and 1895 respectively. France is seen as the most argumentative sight of women's issues. Feminism took its zone out of social consciousness by some active women. There also emerged a group of Proto-feminists who were indirectly supporting feminism evolution in some ways but they nevertheless, didn't consider themselves feminists. If talking in general terms, Feminists fall under three waves encompassing different categories. The feminist movements began first in the West around the nineteenth century, and then it developed towards the east as well as the south.

The first wave of feminism emerged around the 18th century in the West (the United States and the United Kingdom) emphasising to eliminate the slavery of women. Feminist writers of the first wave emphasised women's suffrage and encompassed women's right to education and liberty. It of course focused on women's fundamental rights like a better opportunity for their education, better working condition in their pay scale. It paved the way for Liberal feminist writers. Mary Wollstonecraft's *A Vindication of the Rights of Women* (1792) appeared as the first challenging work of modern feminism that raised the questions of women's right to vote. She was of course the first feminist writer and philosopher who operated the strong ways of women's basic rights focusing on milestones of feminism. She was the first feminist writer who brought into consideration, the discussion of equality of sexes with education, considering education as the most powerful tool for women to fight against unequal established gender disparities. The Liberal feminists believed that all forms of women's sexual discrimination and prejudice will be destroyed through female suffrage.

In the twentieth century, the other female theorist Virginia Woolf came up with her revolutionary theoretical and most argumentative book *A Room Of One's Own* (1929) where she raised the voice of women's freedom in getting education. She focused on the lack of financial opportunities for women. She also advocates equal rights for men and women. Woolf puts her ideas on the great works of Shakespeare and conjectures if there would be a twin sister of Shakespeare, would she have been able to create such legends of English literature? She answers negatively and laments that unequal codes would have been defined for her. Definitely, she would have been strongly thwarted and deprived of getting education. Her observation foregrounds the unpaid money for women's education, the biggest hurdle, which had been running for centuries. Woolf stresses on the equal rights of man and woman between both the sexes. She very much, like the earliest feminist theorist Mary Wollstonecraft takes into account men's biased and cold soldierly nature of men when they categorise women's writing as menial creation.

> A woman's writing is always feminine; it cannot help being feminine; at its best it is most feminine; the only difficulty lies in defining what we mean by feminine.
>
> Virginia Woolf

The second wave of feminism emerged around the 1950s to 1980s. It focussed on gender inequality in laws and culture. A number of prominent feminist writers emerged with their outstanding works like Kate Millet's *Sexual Politics*, Simon de Beauvoir's *The Second Sex,* Shulamith Firestone's *The Dialect of Sex*, Betty Friedan's *The Feminist Mystique,* and Juliet Mitchell's *Women's Estate,* Sheila Rowbotham's *Women's Liberation and the New Politics* and Greer's *The Female Eunuch.* Marxist feminists believed that the factor of class exploitation is a major issue and there is a requirement of modification in the social revolution which will support women's emancipation. They also regarded the development of private property as the basis of the subordination of women. They believed that it's not only women's biological differences and private property that make them different but there are many other factors like, polygamous marriage, economic and political dominance of men, and their complete ruling power over female sexuality which emerged in the form patriarchy. Socialist feminists argue that women face not only political and economic inequality which can be solved by demanding the equal rights of women but the hierarchies between sexes are inherently rooted in social and economic institutions. To speak generally, Socialist feminists acknowledge that the domain of women limited to domestic affairs is an important factor in the economic interest of capitalism. Women generally remain confined to indoor works like child-rearing and carrying the burden of household work which is also a contribution to their family. These works are categorised as unpaid jobs that lead to the economic dependence of women on men. Zillah Eisenstein in *Capitalist Patriarchy and the Case for Socialist Feminism* (1979) has put her ideas, "Male supremacy and capitalism are the core relations that cause the oppression of women. She defines patriarchy as a "sexual system of power in which male possesses superior power and economic privilege". (Eisenstein 1979: 17)

Sylvia Walby in her theoretical work *Patriarchy at Work* (1986) has looked into problems of the patriarchal system. According to her, women remain responsible caring for their children, husband, and other members of the family but such labour is undervalued by their husbands as well as others who dwell in the same family that leads to patriarchy. In the words of Walby, "Patriarchy is a system which consists of social structures and practices, in which men dominate, oppress and exploit women" (214). Patriarchy mostly works as a system of social relations. Patriarchy is composed of six structures: the patriarchal mode of production, patriarchal structures in the state, patriarchal structures in paid work, patriarchal structures in sexuality, patriarchal structures in cultural institutions, such as religion, the media, and education, male violence. It is to be noticed which kind of patriarchy is most brutal for women. (214)

As soon as Radical feminists emerged, they raised the issue of sexual oppression which was the root cause of patriarchy. They believed that unless the system of sexuality is reconstructed women will remain in a subordinate position. Their views lie in the ideology of motherhood that has subjugated women and perpetuated patriarchy (Bhasin 1993: 08). Simon de Beauvoir, in her book *The Second Sex* (1970) says 'one is not born a woman but rather becomes one', that is, women are perceived through social constructs. "While sexual differences are linked to biological differences between male and female, gender differences are imposed socially or even politically by constructed contrasting stereotypes of masculinity and femininity" (de Beauvoir 1970: 258). Beauvoir is absolutely true when she clearly decries patriarchal structures as socially constructed. A 'woman' becomes a 'woman' always under the patriarchal compulsion forced upon them.

Kate Millet, in *Sexual Politics* (1970), argues that men consider politics as power structured relationships through which they control women. Through family, church, and academy, men secure the consent of the women they oppress. Each institution reinforces women's subordination to men with the result that women internalise a sense of inferiority to men. Radical feminists posit that patriarchal oppression is based on gender oppression, and patriarchy gives all power to men to place themselves in all the highest social positions.

The third wave of feminism began around the 1990s after the failure of the second phase. This movement postulated that feminism requires a spirit of revolution and it aimed to trace the position of women pertaining to different races. Feminist writers like Gloria Anzaldua, Chela Sandoval, Bell Hooks, Audre Lorde, Maxine Hong Kingston, and Cherrie Moraga focussed on women's position within the particular community who were victims of racial discrimination. When Alice Walker came up with her revolutionary term 'womanism' in her monumental text *In Search of Our Mother's Garden* (1983), it challenged the traditional nature of patriarchy. She also showed her reaction towards black male writers who stifle the creative instincts of black women. She considers two reasons as to why their black counterparts don't take black women writers' works into serious consideration? The first factor behind it is that she is a woman. Secondly, their male writers regard that these women writers tend to concentrate on familial, domestic, and patriarchal issues and, therefore, black male writers consider their writings to be cliché throwing aside from the list of creative books. (Showalter 1985: 174)

The root of Black feminism (19th Century) is associated with the abolitionist movement of the U.S.A. It was primarily initiated to fight against slavery, and strengthen the position of black women against any form of racial and sexual discrimination. Black feminists consider sexism and racism as important factors of black women's oppression. They point out particular sections of racial, gender, and economic factors that degrade Black women. They have firmly criticised Marxist, Liberal, Socialist and Radical feminists for ignoring 'race' as a category of oppression and exploration. Black feminists believe that women of colour are more vulnerable and more marginalised in comparison to other general women since their 'race' becomes the main tool of oppression. "Black feminism is a process of self-conscious struggle that empowers women and men to actualise a humanist vision of community". (Collins 2000: 39)

Dalit Feminism

The advent of western civilisation became a catalyst for Indians where dalit women remained more vulnerable on the ground of their caste. When British administrators came to India on the pretext of trade, they started making Indians slaves and its effects suppressed more women especially Christian converted dalit women. "It was the material sphere that gave more power to westerners. Science, technology, rational forms of economic organisation, and modern methods of statecraft had given the European countries the strength to dominate the non-European people and to impose their dominance over the whole world" (Chatterjee 1989: 623). After the advent of Western rule, it established lots of ups and downs in the life of Indians. The establishment of print technology encouraged sources of communication, and the general facilities for colonised groups, changing the lifestyle of people. The changing practice of society in the cinema, in public eating places, and education system got moulded into new forms of society; yet it could not eliminate caste discrimination in India; on the contrary, it remained a perpetual social stigma.

The norms of culture invariably keep changing from time to time and the concept of patriarchy is an outcome of such changes. The old order gave way to new changes. The practice which is celebrated in one era is invariably changed in another era bringing the new one. For instance, the Indian society has had a tradition of visiting prostitutes for sexual pleasure. But the beginning of British rule witnessed a change in such occupation during the nineteenth century. So, at that time women who were working at public places whether as prostitutes or other working women, they were considered immoral.

Chatterjee contends that women's questions regarding social and familial position became a central issue in the 19th century. However, by the early 20th century this issue vanished from the public arena. This was primarily because nationalism strongly denied making women's questions an issue of political negotiation with the colonial state. She further argues that the discussions about the promoting works of the middle-class women were put outside the arena of political agitation and the private space was taken as the safe zone of struggles through which nationalist patriarchy established its way to be normalised. Women were taught to be the preservers of tradition. (Rege 1998: 41)

Great personalities like Raja Ram Mohan Roy and Swami Dayanand Saraswati have emerged as strugglers on behalf of women for their equal rights. Raja Ram Mohan Roy continuously fought for civil and political rights castigating strongly until the '*sati*' living-death tradition got abolished. Brahmo Samaj and Arya Samaj founded by Raja Ram Mohan Roy and Dayanand Saraswati proved the active sign of women's freedom. Ranade, the next figure fighting for women's rights founded National Social Conference in 1887 and continued his struggle against a ban on widow-remarriage and child marriage. The British government indeed abolished the menace of the Indian 'sati system' in 1829 but it could not bring a new change for Indian widows because earlier the 'sati' system gave them a quick death with their husbands but even after the abolition of the system, women remained in a vulnerable position. Once the "subject" is gone the "other" can't remain as a single identity, the concept which was in practice in the pre-colonial Indian society is still persistent today in other way and will go on as a perpetuating system. The Christian missionaries allured Dalit women to convert to Christianity on the pretext of free education, wealth, and removal of caste stigma. But converted women became more vulnerable. Later, it evoked in them a sense of protest against these atrocities.

Continuous atrocities on dalits led to a group of social activists like Gautama Buddha, Chokhamela, Mahatma Phule, and later B. R. Ambedkar who made an immense contribution to dalit phenomenon. A majority of them expressed their own views through various political manifestoes and believed that Hindu religious scriptures have deliberately pushed dalits towards the margins through the imposition of certain laws. The word 'dalit' has evolved from the Sanskrit root word 'dal' which highlights a break or a crack. It signifies the subjugation of the marginalised classes by the dominant sections of society through the social hierarchy (cited in Narayan 2006: 34). When Dr. Ambedkar came up with the term "dalit", he strongly rejected the nomenclature "Harijan" given by Mahatma Gandhi which denotes "Children of God or fatherless children". Dr. Ambedkar first time used the term "dalit" for the suppressed as well as exploited people. His main message was "Educate, Organise and Agitate" in order to secure the rights of dalit people. (Rege 2006: 05-11)

When in the twentieth century dalit writers started writing they presented their agonised experiences in their works, they began to define dalit literature in their own way. Nirmalkumar Phadkule articulated his views on dalit literature, "To create Dalit literature, it is not necessary that the writer should be born as untouchable because the basis of Dalit literature does not lie in one's birth in a particular caste. It is a social consciousness" (cited in Singh 2004: 24). According to him, anyone can produce dalit literature who possesses compassion for dalits. But his view on dalit literature has been challenged by Sharankumar Limbale who observes that the particular purpose of Dalit literature is to represent the authentic experiences of dalits. He says that "Dalit literature is a literature which should be written about Dalits, by Dalit writers with a Dalit consciousness" (Limbale 2004: 19). The other Marathi Dalit writer Arjun Dangle delineates Dalit literature saying, dalit literature is nothing but the literary expression of the exploited class. He further goes on to say, "Dalit literature is not simply literature. . . Dalit literature is associated with a movement to bring about change. . . At the very first glance, it will be strongly evident that there is no established critical theory or point of view behind them [i.e. Dalit writings]; instead, there is new thinking and a new point of view". (Dangle 1994 vii-viii)

It is the literature that emboldened dalit subalterns to speak against their resistance, on the blank page. A space where society can read them, know them, give them an identity, and define them. Literature channelised them as speaking subjects unlike history had effaced them. The Hindu society has codified dalit people as 'other'. Sharankumar Limbale castigating the Hindu caste compares dalit consciousness with that of a slave. While some other theorists and critics have strongly compared them with Afro-American race segregated people. But Limbale's definition of dalit in a broad way reflects all the dispossessed and oppressed of India:

> Harijans and neo-Buddhists are not the only Dalits. The term describes all the untouchable communities living outside the boundary of the village, as well as Adivasis, landless farm-labourers, the suffering masses, and nomadic and criminal tribes. In explaining the word, it will not do to refer only to the untouchable castes. People who are lagging behind economically will also need to be included. (Limbale 2004:11)

Dalit literature, in a way, is a rejection of all the tradition, the aesthetics, the romanticism in language against the Brahminical literature that presented dalit men and women as 'other species. When Dalit movement came into existence in the early 20th century, it failed to represent the oppression of dalit women. Noted critic Gopal Guru in his well-known article, "Dalit Women Talk Differently", (1995) argues that dalit women face exclusion not only in the political sphere but also in the cultural field where their literary writings are marginalised by the dalit men as well. Guru aptly contends that it is not only caste and class discrimination but also the issue of gender identity that is one of the vital elements of oppression for dalit women. He defends the independent assertion of dalit women and asserts that Dalit men should not block the developing path of dalit women; rather they should take it positively. Giving them freedom will bring some useful works. Secondly, the autonomous mobility of dalit women also needs to be understood from an epistemological standpoint to make them creative souls so that it will help them in the enhancement of their creative mind. Thus, Dalit women's resentment towards their political and literary marginalisation is a serious point to be noted. (2559)

In the early 1900s, the poignant experience of dalit women provoked them to revolt against their caste and gender-based exploitation and discrimination. Outspoken dalit women like Shivram Janaba Kamble and Santabai became important figures in the Dalit movement of the 20th century in order to eliminate the stigma of prostitution. Even 'The All India Women's Conference' led by Margaret Cousins in 1927 encompassed only urban, English educated middle-class women throwing dalit women at the outskirts of the centre. Vina Mazmudar appeared on the scene in the Women's movement raising the questions of caste and class persisting disparities. The discussion also included the assertion of "widow re-marriage, polygamy". Property rights were also taken into consideration. But it is absolutely disgusting to see that dalit women's rights always remained exempted from mainstream discussion. As we know The Hindu Women's Right of property predominantly showed concern towards higher and middle-class women depriving lower caste women of their basic rights to lead a comfortable marital life.

Rege's survey on dalit women's critical position marks a significant point in her assertion that the widely known movements across the late 1970s and early 1980s, such as the Shramik Mukti Sanghatana, Yuvak Kranti Dal, Satyasodhak Communist Party failed to underscore the rights of dalit women. She further highlights the contribution of the Dalit Panther and Women's movement that were based upon left ideology and foregrounded the autonomous behaviour of women. Although Dalit Panthers movement contributed significantly to the cultural revolt of the 1970s, yet dalit women remained under the threads of 'mother' and the 'victimised sexual objects' in their writings and other programmes. (Rege 1998: 42)

Our great social activist, Jotirao Phule, brought forth his polemical arguments and contended that scriptural authority established by Brahmins in the Hindu society is the cause of all ills for Brahmins as well as non-Brahmins. The Brahminical social structure denied women, Shudras as well as ati-Shudras from attaining the knowledge of scriptures, and forced them to accept the established Brahminical norms. Further E.V. Ramasamy Naicker's Self Reflect Movement appeared as the most powerful political agenda in 1925 and supported the cause of dalit women's welfare by deconstructing the traditional institution of marriage established earlier by Hindu texts which were completely based on the patriarchal system. Due to the commendable contribution of Periyar, the laws of remarriage paved way for the social liberty of dalit women. This movement provided equal rights to divorced men and women. Uma Chakravarti in her theoretical work *Gendering Caste Through a Feminist Lens* (2013) opines that caste system upholds the patriarchal ideologies and values which are used to justify the unequal, hegemonic and dominant patriarchal structures. It needs to pay attention to the marginalisation of women in certain sectors and the structures of society that encourage women subordination (25). Chakravarti posits that the existing system of patriarchy is broadly maintained through multiple social structures.

When the Ambedkarite movement came to prominence in the twentieth century it contributed inordinately to the upliftment of dalit women and enabled them to revolt against oppression. Ambedkar's observation on dalit women's oppression rests on two primary reasons: the caste system and the class system. He asserts that the union of inter-caste marriage and patriarchy proves to be futile for dalit women. In 1927, Dr. Ambedkar's *Satyagraha* movement in Mahad witnessed the active participation of women where they supported the movement actively. The movement claimed the rights of dalits to use water from the general public tank which had been prohibited. Ambedkar particularly focussed on the role of women as nurturers and emphasised the fact that their upliftment is vital for the collective welfare of society. In his speech at Mahad, Ambedkar boosted the morale of dalit women with his thought-provoking words, "Untouchability is a woman's question. You gave birth to us and you know how people grade us and treat us even lower than animals... When you know all this, how would you answer people who will raise questions about why you gave birth to us at all? What is the difference between children born to Kayastha and other savarna women sitting in this meeting and us" (Rege 2006: 54). During another *Satyagraha* event in Nasik (1930), dalit women protested along with Ambedkar against the denial of rights to enter temples.

Brutal incidents of sexual harassment in the 1980s and 1990s became an important issue of concern in the Indian women's movement. A major incident of sexual assault gained widespread attention in 1997 when a marginalised woman Banwari Devi (Kumhar caste) was gang-raped by five people. She was an employee of Rajasthan state-sponsored (WDP) Women's Development's Programme. As a social activist, she advocated the abolition of the institution of child marriage. However, her attempts were fiercely contested by the upper-class people because she was a dalit woman. A Public Interest Litigation (PIL) was filed by a women's organisation against her gang rape in the Supreme Court of India but all efforts proved to be futile. The court failed to dispense adequate measures of justice due to a lack of forensic evidence. On the other side, her husband was restricted from disclosing all the facts. However, Banwari Devi's relentless struggles became evident in her 1995 speech "My struggle is not for myself. It is a collective struggle for all the women who have been wronged. I will continue to fight" (Cited in Gangoli 2007: 96-97). She became the iconic status for all marginalised women. So, it can be said that subaltern women are denied a voice to protest against the crime inflicted upon them. According to Article 17 of the Constitution, caste discrimination has been abolished. Constitutionally caste discrimination has been abolished yet it continues to persist in insidious forms. This caste barrier has particularly proved to be detrimental for dalit women. Vaishali Shiv Kumar has rightly commented in his essay "A Dalit Woman Under a Strong Clutch of Patriarchy" regarding the 'otherness' of Dalit women contends that dalit women always fight against society, and against the traditions where their men rule. It is a naked truth that the threads of patriarchy suppress them, their originality, ability, and even beauty in them.

Literature became a powerful weapon for dalit women to resist the injuries attacked upon them through the androcentric world. They proved Spivak's theory that even the subalterns can speak if they get space to utter their miseries. A leading group of dalit female writers emerged with their literary canons. New literature, in the form of "writings from the margins", came to play a vital role as a mode of articulation for the subalterns, and enabled them to dismantle the old culture hegemony of the center and substitute it with new ones. In India, a great number of female Dalit writers like Bama Faustina, Urmila Pawar, Santabai Kamble, Baby Kamble, P. Sivakami, and Meena Kanadasamy emerged as important figures of literary merit. These dalit feminist writers have strongly attacked the patriarchal threads in their literary genres.

'Gender' vs. 'Writing'

Sex' is generally viewed as a biological term where as 'gender' is a psychological and cultural term" According to the Derridian concept of a phallogocentric system of language, man has been the primary source of authority. Even language is taken as male organised and male creation. A similar view has been reiterated by Lacan who considers discourse as phallogocentric, and says that language is always male-dominated. Lacan, the French psychoanalytic ensures us that when a child enters into symbolic order from mother recognition, a child's language rests based on the oedipal phase in which the child accepts his or her gender identity. This stage brings us to examine the acceptance of phallus as certain privileged signification and after all the exclusion of females from center. In the words of Cora Kaplan, this symbolic stage of a child is recognised as follows:

> The phallus as a signifier has a central, crucial position in language, for if language embodies the patriarchal law of the culture, its basic

> meanings refer to the recurring process by which sexual difference and subjectivity are acquired. . . .Thus the little girl's access to the Symbolic, i.e. to the language and its laws, is always negative and/or mediated by intro-subjective relation to a third term, for it is characterised by identification with lack.

Feminist writers like Virginia Woolf, Helen Cixous, Julia Kristeva, Sandra Gilbert, and Susan Gubar resist men's such an ideology of 'language as male-oriented and male centred'. Gilbert and Gubar jointly define the hierarchal structures that divide women's writing on gender basis milestones of literary paternity through the work, *The Madwoman in the Attic.* They further argue in a wider sense, "the text's author is a father, a progenitor, a procreator, an aesthetic patriarch whose pen is an instrument of generative power like his penis". Women lack phallic authority through which they are devalued. They go on harshly castigating on men's ideas on phallocentric theory, women's writing is profoundly marked by the anxieties of this gender disparity: If the pen is a metaphorical penis, from what organ can females generate texts?".

Helen Cixous and Monique Witting reach at the same research when they say that through the process of 'phallus' a man defines the world as a 'unified' center of the universe. Both feminist critics interpret; such ideology has been accepted not only by religion and philosophy but also by language. Men dominate the world through the mastery of language-oriented authority. Men as mainstream dominate the world through verbal mastery that is called symbolic discourse. By this specific discourse man as a center objectifies the world, speaks in the place of everything and everyone else---including women. Such patrilineal threads were established everywhere for example myths, rituals, speech, writing as well as all religious organisations and it is not only problematic but far and far difficult to break religious organisations' codified patriarchal systems.

Cixous and Irigaray have rightly pointed out here the historical status of women. They both assert strongly on the historical portrayal of women as sexual objects and sexual pleasure for men. There is no denying in this fact that women historically have been presented sometimes in some abusive words. Their freedom of expression of sexuality have been restricted by the patriarchal culture of society. Now it's time when they should go against such a phallogocentric concept. If they break it with a new language, there will emerge a different site of difference from which phallogocentric concepts and controls will be seen apart, not only in theory but also in practice.

Julia Kristeva, a semiotic – Marxist through her critical term 'semiotic discourse' regards that men's writing language is rooted in a historical concept where their structuring texts rules and regularities are accepted as a conventional language. In Kristeva's views, women also like any other man speak and write as 'hysterics' as male-dominated discourse. She further extends two reasons why they can write like men; first, the predominance in them of drives associated with childbirth and so their marginal position is set opposite to masculine. In a society, the sexual and symbolic context of being a woman always assigns a means to another end, to becoming something else: a subject-in-the-making, a subject on trial. She goes on to say that women instead of formulating a new discourse, should resist challenging the discourses that stand in their way. "If a woman has a role to play. . . it is only in assuming a negative function; they should strongly reject everything that embodies finite, structured, definite, loaded with meaning already existing modes of society. Such male-oriented structures throw women aside on the side of the explosion of social codes: with revolutionary movements" (363). So, in the views of Kristeva women represent not so much a sex as an attitude, any resistance to conventional culture and language; men, too, have access to the *jouissance* that opposes phallogocentrism:

> A feminist practice can only be . . . at odds with what already exists so that we may say "that's not it" and "that's still not it". By "women" I mean that which cannot be represented, what is not said, what remains above and beyond nomenclatures and ideologies. There are certain "men" who are familiar with this phenomenon. (Showalter 1985: 363)

Luce Irigaray another feminist on the contrary asserts her notions, women have a specificity that distinguishes them sharply from men. Like any other feminist Irigaray too makes her argument saying that women have no way of knowing and representing themselves only because they have been entrapped in a world that is built upon man-centered. Women have been misinterpreted in 'body' through male discourse. She argues that female sexuality explains women's problematic relationship to (masculine) logic and language:

> Woman has sex organ just about everywhere. She experiences pleasure almost everywhere. . . . The geography of her pleasure is much more diversified, more multiple in its differences, more complex, more subtle, than is imagined---in an imaginary [system] centered a bit too much on one and the same. "She" is infinitely other in herself. That is undoubtedly

> the reason she is called temperamental, incomprehensible, perturbed, capricious---not to mention her language in which "she" goes off in all directions and in which "he" is unable to discern the coherence of any meaning. Contradictory words seem a little crazy to the logic of reason, and inaudible for him who listens with ready-made grids, a code prepared in advance. In her statements---at least when she dares to speak out---woman retouches herself constantly. (cited in Showalter 1985: 364)

Irigaray asserts that women's discovery of their autoeroticism will not, by itself, arrive automatically or enable them to transform the already existing ideology. "For a woman to arrive at the point where she can enjoy her pleasure as a woman, a long detour by the analysis of the various systems that oppress her is certainly necessary". (364)

Some radical feminist critics like Rich react harshly against the ideologies that believe that a biological difference in the writing process. They argue that women's writing is thought as a creation from a bodily point of view that functions invariably from men's body. The sexual difference is also a major issue in the reign of the writing process. Rich in her critical work *In Of Woman Born* clearly explains the linchpins of feminine bodily differences:

> Female biology . . . has far more radical implications than we have yet come to appreciate. Patriarchal thought has limited female biology to its own narrow specifications. The feminist vision has recoiled from female biology for these reasons; it will, I believe, come to view our physically as a resource rather than a destiny. In order to live a fully human life, we require not only control to our bodies . . . we must touch the unity and resonance of our physicality, the corporeal ground of our intelligence.

Even the great philosopher Aristotle aptly states, "The natural dichotomy between ruler and being ruled, the soul is by nature the ruler, the body the subject. He propounds that the male is always superior and the female inferior and so the one rules and the other is ruled; this principle is applied to all mankind". He further says:

> If, then, the male stands for the effective and active, and the female, considered as female, for the passive, it follows that what the female would contribute to the semen of the male would not be semen but material for the semen to work upon. This is just what we find to be the case, for the catamenia have in their nature an affinity to the primitive matter. (Cited in Lerner 1986: 208)

According to Aristotle, man alone is powerful and creator of everything. He has creative power which woman loses. He regards males as *homo faber,* the maker who has his own mind to design any work in a lasting form. He also believes in the concept that it is the biological inferiority in women that makes them inferior to man in thinking capability and production. They lack somewhere or else reasoning power.

Plato the teacher of Aristotle considers private property as the root cause of patriarchal authority. Private property should be abolished through its all ways because private property engenders class disparities and disharmony. Hence men and women should have common leading ways of life-----common education, common rights, and common privileges that will organise a common life for them. Although Aristotle agreed on Plato's body vs. soul dualism, as well as natural inequality between both the sexes and the justice of the stronger one over the weaker one but he was not fully susceptible to the ideas of Plato and Socrates regarding women. That's why his ideas differ a little from Socrates and Plato. Aristotle's viewpoints rationalise the exclusion of women from the political arena which is the core of the foundation of the democratic world. Aristotle's views are based on Biblical fallen Eve that helped in the establishment of patriarchal dominance. While Socrates proposes to contradict views from Aristotle on men-women sex when he says that women should be given the same opportunity, freedom of expression and same privileges as men enjoy. He emphasises strongly on differences of education between both the sexes. Women are kept deprived of getting good education opportunities. We should continue to maintain equal opportunities for daughters and wives.

Plato and Freud refer to women in the symbolic forms of irrational and invisible, as imperfect and incomplete. If we see through the eyes of our noted psychological theorist Sigmund Freud we find how he takes a rather negative remark in the assessment of women. He identifies men with active control of power and females with passivity. He regards sperm and penetration as the active part, while vaginal reception and ova as the passive. He further asserts that women are incapable of contributing to civilisation due to weaker sexual instincts. According to him, the penis signifies human progress and moral understanding and contributes to the development of art and civilisation. In Freud's views, women are inherently subservient, and males dominant, more strongly sexed, and therefore entitled to sexually subjugate the female because as a female she deserves such oppression. He interprets women's sex as inherently inferior and it can never be given superior status. He utters that like race, sex is something one cannot really change. For sexuality, he has sketched out women as being attacked through male penis while women while receiving sperm remain to lie in a passive position. (Cited in Millet 1988: 170-181)

If we examine feminist studies in depth we find that sexuality in women that our world distinctly identifies it from men is not innate quality in women or men but it is developed through the individual's encounters with the nuclear family or to say the way parents bring up differentiating according to their sex. Juliet Mitchell correctly describes that in our society girls in their infancy phase shift their love between father and mother and ultimately in this process they develop a sense of their own anatomy that they observe clearly is socially less valued than that of boys. Lacanian theory of 'Symbolic' also denotes that a girl child identifies the symbolic value attributed to the phallus where she incorporates and fits herself comfortably into the phallocentric world through her father's language. In a way, we can say that early gender identity determines her 'other' that is called the second gender. Gender is not a natural given but rather it is the epitome of social interactions that represent them through some symbols and signs. Nancy Chodorow's interpretations concerning gender discrimination in her text *The Production of Mothering: Psychoanalysis and the Sociology of Gender* tells us the discriminated upbringing of children within the family since the earliest period. Boys, in order to find their distinct identity themselves with the father rather than their mother who are categorised 'others' than father. She further claims that it is women who nurture children, and men; so there is a need for some reform in the way mothers behave discriminately with the girls. She explicitly stands with her ideas:

> Boys are taught to be masculine more consciously than girls are taught to be feminine. . . The feminine identification that a girl attains and the masculine identification about which a boy remains uncertain are valued differently. . . A girl identifies with and is expected to identify with her mother in order to attainher adult feminine identification and learn her gender adult gender role. (Chodorow 1978: 176-177)

CHAPTER 3

Evolution of Caste and Untouchability

Ambedkarite Movement

Dr. Ambedkar was the most prominent figure of dalit reformation. He had to undergo so many tortures and humiliation owing to caste stigma. While studying law he came to know that every law was completely based on upper caste people's law and they were manipulating marginalising the backward, tribals, and the schedule caste people. Such people were being deprived of knowing their fundamental rights. Dr. Ambedkar could recognise the monopoly of caste politics when he studied deeply books concerning the law and rights of all people.

When Ambedkar was invited to deliver his speech in The Jat-Pat-Todak Mandal in Lahore in 1935, he had prepared a long speech that was based on Brahmanism that is a Hindu caste system. He was appalled when his name was withdrawn from the conference. The reason behind it was clear that he wanted to eradicate persisting caste atrocities, untouchability, and class disparity that were a toxic element for social welfare. Fighting with the law he was adamant to participate in the conference and to put his motivational speech before Hindu society. He didn't like to participate in a movement that was carrying the threads of the Hindu caste system. But his attempt proved a failure because he could not get the opportunity to deliver his thoughts from the presidential chair so the public also lost the opportunity to understand his views on the problems created by the Hindu caste system. But eventually, he got his manuscript in Bombay and that led to a controversy among Hindu people.

In his, *The Annihilation of Caste* Dr. Ambedkar has clearly disclosed the hypocritical attitudes of the Hindu caste system. It was a fact that the condition of untouchables was pathetic under the rule of Peshwas in Maratha country. The untouchables were prohibited from using the public roads if a Hindu was passing across the same road because a mere shadow of untouchables was pollution for them. The untouchables were expected to tie a black thread either on his wrist or around his neck because it symbolised a sign to save the Hindus from getting themselves polluted by the untouchable's touch by mistake.

In Poona also the untouchables were asked to carry an earthen pot hung around their neck wherever they went around for holding their spit, lest their spit falling on the earth pollute a Hindu man. They had to carry a broom to sweep away from behind them the dust they trod on, lest a Hindu walking behind them on the same road be polluted. Dr. Ambedkar was extremely troubled at the codes imposed upon untouchables. As he describes such codes in *The Annihilation of Caste* (1936). The untouchables were not allowed to wear gold-lace-bordered *pugrees*. They were prohibited from wearing dhotis with coloured or fancy borders. They were assigned the job to spread the death-news of any Hindu to the relatives of the deceased. And during upper-caste Hindu marriage, these untouchables were expected to play music before the procession. Untouchable women were prohibited from wearing gold or silver ornaments; they must not wear fancy gowns or jackets. They were expected to render services without demanding remuneration and must accept whatever a Hindu is pleased to give them. And if they would reluctant in following the Hindu assigned codes, they had no alternate except leaving the village. (12)

So, in this way, the untouchables were prohibited from even eating delicious food or using ghee in their feast because 'ghee' was the sign of upper caste people's status. Even if an untouchable person could afford it but he was not allowed to use 'ghee' in his food. In any way, there was not a single sign of freedom for untouchables. Their every step of life was controlled through Hindu Brahminical system order. Rousseau's philosophy is very much applicable to the untouchable people when he says, "Man is born free but he is everywhere in a chain". Untouchables are everywhere fettered through Brahminical reign. Caste stigma hurdles them everywhere whether it is the educational platform or professional platform. It is like everlasting stigma from which it is very problematic to recuperate. In the words of Dr. Ambedkar, "There cannot be a more degrading system of social organisation than the caste system. It is the system which deadens, paralyses, and cripples the people, [keeping them] from helpful activity" (28). Dr. Ambedkar further tells us historical ample evidences of caste as a barrier. There was only one period that was during the Mourya Empire when the country had evidence of annihilation of the caste system and when the *Shudras* led their own life and became the rulers of the country. But apart from this period, the caste system was deep-rooted in all periods. And Dr. Ambedkar calls the period of defeat and darkness as such a period when the caste system flourished, to the damnation of the greater part of the people of the country.

Hindu society was running through the established Brahminical *Chaturvarnya* structured system. According to *Chaturvarnya,* there are four main classes: *Brahmin, Kshatriya, Vaishya*, and *Shudra.* It classified their work: that the Brahmins should cultivate knowledge, the *Kshatriya* should bear arms, and the *Vaishya* should trade while the Shudra should serve all the three, as it sounds like the division of labour according to the class. Women remained excluded from the *Chaturvarnya* system. Their status was tied with their husband. This system ruined women's own particular identity and instead bound accordingly the consequences of marriage. It was the codes of *Chaturvarny*a that continued to maintain its suffocating conspiracy against women and *shudras.* That's during the writing of the *Ramayana* women and shudras were thrown from Chaturvarnya. During Ram Raj, *Chaturvarnya* was in full practice. Rama had killed Shambuka only because Shambuka was a *Shudra* who was transgressing his class status to be a Brahmin. On the other hand, Rama as a ruler had to maintain the system of Chaturvarnya so how could he let it go unnoticed. And later that's why *Manusmriti* prescribed a heavy sentence as cutting off the tongue or pouring of molten lead in the ears of the shudras if ever by mistake they hear the Veda. The same codes became applicable for women regarding reciting or hearing Veda.

The propounders of *Chaturvarnya* believed in the concept that why should *Shudras* trouble acquiring wealth when the three upper Varnas are there to support them? According to *Chaturvarnya, Shudras* should not worry about getting an education when there are Brahmins to whom they can approach for reading and writing. The principles of *Chaturvarnya* were established deeply rooted to put *Shudras* as the ward and where all the other three appeared as a head. And Indian people who have blind faith in religious norms led them to follow these stupid theories without objecting to its man-made suffocating rules to suppress *shudras*. There is no denying fact that *Chaturvarnya* was built to enslave *Shudras,* it was like master and servant, oppressor and oppressed, lord and beggar. The three *Varnas* jointly united together to throw Shudras from the centre to the pile of margins. It was the conspiracy behind the principles of *Chaturvarnya* to deprive *Shudras* of achieving education lest they will defeat them one day once they come to know their rights and then it will lead them to be independent of upper *Varnas. Shudras* were strongly prohibited from bearing arms, lest they should have the means to rebel against their deprived authority. *Brahmins* knew that 'knowledge is power' so once the Shudras achieve knowledge they will own their power.

Owning to the prevalent caste system, *Shudras* never got the opportunity to change their lower job as labourers, ploughman, hunter, herdsman, sweepers, and many other lower-class jobs which the upper three Varna people never preferred. They were not given the opportunity to rise up and develop their mind-set. Social war between the strong and the weak has been historically a toxic practice where the strong one inevitably dominates over the weaker one. As we see Europe being the most economically powerful country has been dominating over all other countries and the rest of the countries always live under constant fear. So is the case with caste politics in our country where the upper castes have been dominating over the lower castes. The structure of cultural power is what Marxist theorist Antonio Gramsci called 'cultural hegemony' through which dominant classes manipulated the culture of powerless society economically and culturally, and where the imposed world view of the ruling class became the words of scriptures; their imposed political, as well as cultural norms, got justified that eventually led to social, economic and political marginalisation of the masses. Even the other Marxist theorist Mitchell Foucault gave the concept that 'power is everywhere' and 'knowledge is power'. One who possesses the knowledge, the weapon of power is with him. Our Nineteenth-century Darwinian theory also tells us "survival of the fittest" is prevalent everywhere. In the world of a battle between the stronger and weaker, only those who have power survive and get the victory.

Dr. Ambedkar was also depressed due to Mahatma Gandhi's belief in *Chaturvarnya.* Actually, Mahatma Gandhi belonged to a Baniya family. But later his family left the ancestral business in favour of ministership, as it was need of Brahmanism. He studied law and never came in contact with a trade that was his ancestral business. The question here arises that if he believed in *Chaturvarnya* then why didn't he himself stick to the ancestral business of trade as the rules of Chaturvarnya says. He believed in the caste system and so he defended Brahminical orthodoxies. He blindly had firm faith in the *Vedas*, the *Puranas,* and the *Upnishads* that are completely built upon Hindu law. In his views, Verna is based on the principle of each according to his worth, while caste is based on the principle of each according to his birth. So, by this theory, he believed only in the caste system. But even behind this theory, there was some politics which he was masking of changing from ancestral business and getting entrance into politics. He never wanted *shudras* to develop, that's why he was troubled on the concept of inter-dining, inter-drinking, and inter-marrying. He never liked mixing between shudras and non-shudras.

Dr. Ambedkar could perceive Mahatma's monopoly and attacked his political conspiracy. Ambedkar strongly spread his principle against Mahatma questioning inter-marriage and inter-dinning. "Caste is not a physical object like a wall of bricks or a line of barbed wire which prevents the Hindus from co-mingling and which has, therefore, to be polluted down. Caste is a notion, it is a state of mind. The destruction of caste does not, therefore, mean the destruction of a physical barrier. It means a notional change" (Ambedkar 1936: 31). He appeals to all people not to believe in Hindu Shastras because it is the main root of oppression and humiliation for dalits on the basis of caste. People will not change their orthodoxical Hindu beliefs until they cease to adhere to the sanctity of the Hindu Shastras on which their conscience is built upon. He further extends his motivational words in religious threads:

> So long as people look upon it as religion they will not be ready for a change, because the idea of religion is generally speaking, not associated with the idea of change. But the idea of law is associated with the idea of change, and when people come to know that what is called religion is really Law, old and archaic, they will be ready for a change, for people know and accept that can be changed. (37)

After a big tumult in caste politics in 1935, Dr. Ambedkar had lost all hopes of reforming Hinduism from within. He had completely fed up after Brahminical roots seemed adamant to be eliminated. As he said, "Now we come to the constitution that there is no change in the attitude of the Touchables and they are not ready to behave with us with affection, despite our continuous struggle. As such we have decided to remain separate from Hindus, to live with self-help, and struggle to attain self-elevation" (Jadhav 2014: 202). Once again he presided over the Yeola Conference, the same day (13th October 1935) where a vast crowd of Untouchables participated. After delivering a warm speech over an hour and a half, he pointed out the plight of the Depressed Classes in all fields like social, educational, political, and economic. He also raised the question over the Kalaram Temple Entry Movement wherein Untouchables were severely treated out inhumanely over the past five years. He was upset realising that all the money spent on and efforts made to achieve the objectives proved futile and meaningless. He was trying hard to fetch the Untouchables to the centre where there was no mark of presence for them. He was constantly trying hard to bring a new change among the Untouchables in the caste discriminated society but the Upper castes were not budging over this crucial issue what the country needed. A wave of changing the religion came to his mind and to give up Hinduism. He thought it would be better if I give up Hinduism and embrace another faith that would universally give me equal status.

He then announced his strategy to change the religion publicly. Subsequently, he exhorted the Untouchables if they wished to convert the religion and leave Hinduism as there is no worst religion other than Hinduism. He asked his people to stop now the battle for Kalaram Temple *Satyagraha* and be separate from the Hindu community. His decision appeared like a tornado over the entire country. It was like a sudden shock among the Hindu community who never wanted him to uprise. The Hindu politicians started commenting on this stunt. His own people took him as messiah while others called it a suicidal step. Gandhiji could not help commenting and making a derogatory remark on Ambedkar's decision of covert:

> I can understand the anger of a high-souled and highly educated person like Dr. Ambedkar over atrocities such as were committed in Kavitha and other villages. But religion is not like a house or a clock which can be changed at will. It is more an integral part of one's own self, rather than of the body. Religion is the tie that binds one to one's creator and whilst the body perishes and it is the religion that persists even after death. If Dr. Ambedkar has any faith in God, I would urge him to assuage his wrath and reconsider his position and examine his ancestral religion on its own merits and not through the weakness of its own merits and not through the weakness of its unfaithful followers. . .

> Lastly, I am convinced, change of faith by him, and those who passed the resolution would not serve the cause which they have at heart; for the millions of unsophisticated illiterate. Harijans would not listen to him especially when it is remembered that their lives for good or evil are intertwined with those of caste Hindus. (203-204)

Gandhi's comments on religion could not affect Dr. Ambedkar's decision over changing the religion. He responded to the words of Gandhiji, "what religion we shall belong is not thought out, but we have decided one thing, and that after due deliberations and with deep conviction, that Hindu religion is not good for us since it is based on equality" (204). He further extended his views in long statements:

> Let no one think I have done this in a huff, or as a matter of wrath against the treatment meted out to the Depressed Classes at Kavitha village or any other place. It is a deeply deliberated decision. I agree with Gandhiji that religion is necessary, but I don't agree that man should have his ancestral religion if he finds that religion is repugnant to his notions of the sort of religion he needs as a standard for his own conduct and as a source of inspiration for his advancement and well-being. (204)

Dr. Ambedkar was pained thinking over that in our country no politician cares for the poverty and the suffering of marginalised people. Even if some people help others only selecting the people of their own caste and own people. This is a complete pervert sense of people. No religion tells us that we should only care for people of our own caste and not others but it is the conservative mindset of Hinduism that thwarts depressed class people. Only the Hindu religion is based on caste and class. This religion does not know how to respect human beings. Everyone is independent to lead his life own way. Christianity and Islam never believe in the concept of untouchability and class disparity. Both the religions contain a sense of humanity for others. But Hindu religion is completely bereft of humanity. Dr. Ambedkar was in a huff perceiving what's the use of such a religion which doesn't maintain a sense of equality and humanity and so it is of no worth in clinging to such a religion? He requested all the depressed class people gathering in the conference to convert the religion to Buddhism which doesn't know inequality and untouchability. So long as they remain Hindu, they can't bring reform in political safeguard; they can't get their fundamental rights of living free. Unless they take some initiative in political safeguard; unless they liberate themselves from the serfdom of Hindu society, their torturous life will persist apace. So, looking at all the crux of atrocities, there is an urgent need for change in religion as well as conscience. Even though conversion does not bring any harm to their fundamental rights of leading an independent life. If they want political safeguard, they must convert their religion. Even though they concert their religion their political, as well as human rights, will remain standstill. Conversion is a need for all rounds whether it is spiritual or worldly gain.

Dr. Ambedkar castigating Hindu orders interprets that man is not for religion; religion is for man. It is urgent to change religion if Untouchables want to become human. He then puts his own decision publicly concerning his own conversion:

> To get organised, convert yourselves. To achieve strength, convert yourselves. To secure equality, convert yourselves. To get liberty, convert yourselves. To make domestic life happy, convert yourselves. Why do you remain in that religion which does not treat you as human beings? Why do you remain in that religion which does not allow you to be educated? Why do you remain in that religion which prohibits you from entering a temple? Why do you remain in that religion which prohibits you from taking water? Why do you remain in that religion which obstructs you from getting a job? Why do you remain in such a religion which insults you at every step?
>
> What message I should give you on this occasion, I take refuge in the words of Gautama Buddha: "Be your own guide. Take refuge in your own reason. Do not listen to the advice of others. Do not succumb to others. Be truthful. Take refuge in truth. Never surrender to anything". For myself, I have already taken a decision. My conversion is for sure. My conversion is not for any material gain. Nothing but spirituality is at the core of my conversion. The Hindu religion does not appeal to my reason. The Hindu religion does not appeal to my self-respect. However, for you, conversion is a must for spiritual as well as material gain. (212)

After his motivational speech at the conference, a large crowd of Untouchables especially people of his *Mahar* community decided to convert to Buddhism. Ambedkar's campaign was a major step to the upliftment of depressed class people. Following his footsteps, a large majority of 400,000 converted to Buddhism in 1956.

A Discussion on the History of 'Origin of Shudras and Untouchables'

There has been a mystery why *shudras* were pushed to the lowest category. Why did the Brahmanic view put them outside the mainstream Varna? The *Purusha Shukta* which is regarded as a theory of the origin of the Universe classifies four classes. It is obvious from the verses of 11 and 12 of *Purusha Shukta* that the four classes respectively are divided with their separate works: *Brahmins* or priests; *Kshatriya* or soldiers; *Vaishyas* or traders; and *Shudras* or menials; emerged from the body of Creator. It put the *Brahmin* to be above all, the *Kshatriya* below the *Brahmin* but above the *Vaishya* and the Shudra; the *Vaishya* below the Kshatriya but above the Shudra; and the *Shudra* lowest of all. But *Purusha Shukta* seems completely contrast not only to other assumptions but also the *Rig Veda* verdict. When we go back to the *Rig Veda* we have clear-cut evidence of class-free society. It does not give importance to class division while the *Purusha Shukta* is beyond such ideology. It manifests the stereotypical division of classes that is the creation of men's minds and nothing else.

The ideologies of the *Purusha Shukta* played a toxic role in propounding the theory of *Chaturvarnya.* It further paves the way for the stereotypical existence of four classes in the Indo-Aryan society. The principles rooted in the *Purusha Shukta* being anti-social were in a way to criminalise the society because its objective was to perpetuate unequal class conflicts, a sort of unjust infliction upon the weaker and marginalised class of people. *Chaturvarnya* unfolded the rise of the fifth class that was next below the *Shudras.* It invented later some incongruous terms, such as *Savarnas, Avarnas, Dvijas, non-Dvijas*, and *Traivernikas.* The *Savarna* included *Brahmins, Kshatriyas, Vaishyas,* and *Shudras*; while the Untouchables or ati-Shudras were called *Avarnas.* So, Chaturvarnya encompassed *Brahmins, Kshatriyas, Vaishyas,* and *Shudras* while the Untouchables or the *ati-Shudras* were put outside the *Chaturvarnya.* This all man-made book allowed special rights to upper caste people. The *Brahmins, Kshatriyas, Vaishyas* were given the right to wear the sacred thread. Logically they were Dvijas. And the *Shudras* and *ati-Shudras* were deprived to have right of wearing the same sacred thread as they were non-Dvijas. If *Chaturvarnya* takes *Brahmins, Kshatriyas, Vaishyas,* and *Shudras* within *Savarna* then the question here haunts us why *Shudras* were denied the right of the *Traivernikas*? It reflects the riddle of *Chaturvarnya.*

The ancient Brahminical concepts evidently denote that the origin of the four classes was unjustified and immoral socially and hence the place of the *Shudras* was assigned very unnatural. It is vague to tell the authenticity of such Hindu religious books. Some historians and scholars allege that *Purusha* sole was the origin of the four *Vernas;* some allege Brahma as its creator; some consider to Prajapati and some to Vratya. Different people give their different notions, different explanations, and observations. All still keep wandering in the world of fantasy or imagination as there is no prevailing truth behind such theories. All such speculations really and explicitly are the frameworks of idiots and man-made. It is very difficult to assume it as real without the thread of factual history.

If we turn back we obviously find that Brahmins as law-makers assigned unjust penalties to the *Shudras*. It's an absolutely striking question why only the *Shudra* alone has been targeted by the Brahmanic law-makers as a victim and not *Vaishya*? Why Brahmins targeted only the *Shudras* to maintain their law-making authority? The reason is simple that the *shudras* were deprived of all the human rights. Brahminical Law imposed certain severe rules for the *Shudras* not only for the short term but permanently. It made a law that *shudras* can't citeVedas or even hear and if they go against this Brahminical man-made law their tongue would be cut to pieces and molten lead would be poured into their ear without a delay. This severe punishment refers to Brahminical orthodox and atrocities towards the Shudras. This system is nothing except a strategy to maintain Brahminical authorial power. Brahmins knew that if they keep the shudras aside from the Vedas and Shastras, and gaining education, they will never be aware of their human rights and so they will never try to excavate the conspiracy of Brahminical truth.

Shudras vs. Aryans

The way Brahmins have presented Shudras in the historical and Hindu religious it's vague. No Brahmanic writers give clear proof of how Shudras came to be called the fourth Verna and how even some Shudras became ati-Shudras. The people who created the Vedic literature primarily belonged to the Aryan race. Now the question here arises who were Aryans and how they advented in India? The English word 'Aryan' is borrowed from the Sanskrit word *'arya'* which signifies "noble" or "noble one". The Aryan race no doubt came from Iran and invaded India when India was passing through turmoil. The natives of our country were called *Dasas* and *Dasyus* since they were a dark race while Aryans were a white race and so racially different from our native people. The Aryans being powerful attacked our country explicitly and defeated our native people. And in the battle, the Aryans conquered the *Dasas* and *Dasyus*. The conquered *Dasas* and *Dasyus* were enslaved and then called enslaved people, Shudras. The Shudras were of course the non-Aryan original inhabitants of India in the form of primitive and a savage state of civilisation. The Aryans formed the colour prejudices and took the support of Chaturvarnya to establish the firm authority over the enslaved native people of our country. Although some scholars say that there is no evidence of any invasion by the Aryans in the Vedas. The Vedas don't reveal that the Aryans were different in colour from the *Dasas* and *Dasyus*. But the certain verses of the Rig Veda expose clearly that there were two different races of Aryans who were inimical to each other. The question here is why there is the sacred character of the different values. Why was the Rig Veda regarded as sacred and why was the Atharva Veda as vulgar? Its simple answer is that the two belonged to separate races of Aryans. And when they became one the Atharva Veda came to be regarded on a par with the Rig Veda. The entire Brahminical law is based on two controversial versions. One refers to a human being, Manu, as the progenitor while the other one refers to God Brahma or Prajapati as the originator. One is regarded as historical while the other one as supernatural. One elaborately explains the four Vernas while the other one focuses on the explanation of the origin of society alone.

The main question here strikes us whether the *Purusha Shukta* is a later composition that was added to the original Rig Veda. The other point is that had the *Purusha Shukta* an old text, other Vedas would have got the main focus of liberty. Whatever may be the truth but one thing is clear from study that *Purusha Shukta* is a stereotypical ideology built upon Brahminical concepts to boost up the claim of Brahmanism authority. On the basis of such conjectural ideas, we have two distinct types of the invention of *Chaturvarnyas*. Supernatural *Chaturvarnya* is attributed to Purusha who carved its principles. And while the other *Chaturvarnya* is regarded as natural *Chaturvarnya* developed among Manu's sons. Here the two controversial existence of two separate *Chaturvarnya* create the different ideologies; it means distinct ideologies of two different Aryan races – one believing in Chaturvarnya and the other not believing in *Chaturvarnya* – and ultimately both merged and became one.

The question also strikes us why only *Shudras* became the fourth *Verna*? Of course, the Shudras were degraded to that position and it was not like that they were originally born as *Shudras*. It is clear evidence from research that the Shudras were degraded in between the conflict between the *Shudras* and the Brahmins. Our history is evident that a great violence took place between the *Shudra* king, Sudas, and the Brahmin Rishi Vasistha. As history says Vasistha and Vishvamitra who were *Kshatriya* were strong enemies. The dispute between duo occured on the following points:

a) The right to receive gifts.

b) The right to teach the Vedas (the Kshatriya had only the right to study the Vedas. He had no right to teach Vedas).

c) The right to officiate at a sacrifice (Kshatriya had the right to perform sacrifices, but he had no right to officiate as a priest at a sacrifice).

In between the battle of a duel between Vasistha and Vishvamitra, Sudas the *Shudra* played a vital role. Actually, Vasistha was a family priest of Sudas. It was Vasistha who helped him to win the battle against the ten kings. And the other side Sudas defeated Vasistha from office. But in his place, he appointed Vishvamitra as his *purohita.* This is for the first time a conflict between Sudas and Vasistha took place. Later incident discloses that Sudas threw Shakti, the son of Vasistha into the fire and burned him alive. This story lies in Satyayana Brahmana. Historical conflict between Brahmins and *Shudras* created a new history. Eventually, due to the conflict between the Brahmins and *Shudra, Shudras* came to be degraded to the fourth Verna.

Why Marginalised People became 'Untouchables'?

The origin of untouchability lies much earlier in history as there is no perfect evidence of it. But only on the basis of an assumption, we introspect over its root. A vast number of scholars have deconstructed the history of 'untouchability' according to their researches.

To speak in general terms, untouchability refers to the notion of pollution, defilement, contamination and simultaneously it includes all the words that signify 'humiliation' and 'impurity'. Such notions of defilement and pollution have been rooted in the Primitive era since Primitive people also have been carrying such concepts of defilement and pollution of *Shudras.* If we see through the lens of Dr. Ambedkar's text "*The Untouchables: Who Were they and Why they Became Untouchables* 'human body' we find a clear-cut picture of the origin of Untouchability. It is Hindu Brahminical texts that have imposed such concepts of defilement or pollution to marginalise the Shudras. As

Manu's statement reveals the conservative mind-set of the Hindu caste system when he states, Brahmins were' ever pure'. This statement is enough to analyse the glorified sense of Brahmanism.

Besides the individual defilement, the Hindu caste system also believes in Communal pollution and purification. It signifies the rooted sense of untouchability in the entire community of the lower castes. It states, the untouchables are born impure, and even the children they procreate are assigned with the stigma of 'untouchability'. And so even the coming generation after generation they will constantly remain impure. It is not merely a social phenomenon that can last for a temporary period. It is an eternal stigma which nothing can cleanse or purify. It is a practice of territorial segregation and imprisoning the untouchable people inside the demarcated position that is a sort of cage. Any violation against the social codes brings severe punishment for them. It shows the inherent feature of untouchability practiced by the Hindu system.

If we turn to history we come to know how the untouchables were put outside the centre. The problems arise with the conflict between settlers and settled people. As we know evidently that primitive society was a nomadic centered. They kept wandering from place to place for a long time. Gradually they started learning the art of cultivating land, farming. And accumulating wealth from cattle to land brought a tremendous change in their unstable position of some nomadic. Having such change the Primitive society became stable. But subsequently there confronted two classes – one called Broken men and the other settled people. All Nomadic tribes could not become settled ones. They were always at war. They did realise that the settled nomadic group was getting doubly wealthy. Definitely, the settled groups were possessing cattle like the nomadic group but the settled had also grown corn and land which the nomadic group now lacked. Furthermore, the settled tribes remained engaged in agriculture. But it is really a serious matter that even that settled tribe could not develop their brain to convert ploughs into swords. It had been a continuous warfare in the life of the Primitive tribes. In the Primitive society, every individual inevitably belonged to a tribe and there was no existence of people outside the tribe. In the conflict of war, the settled and the Broken tribes became a divided group. The Broken Men had eventually to be separate from the settled one, aside the village. They remained vulnerably with a fear of who would attack them and when it was not certain. They were confronting the problems of shelter and protection.

Although the Broken men had had a blood relationship with the settled group but after the warfare, they became marginalised group and lived with the stigma of 'untouchability'. So, it is clear from the research that the Untouchables were originally the Broken men who got defeated due to lack of land and corn. Since they were Broken men so they were ostracised from the centre to the margins and were allowed to live outside the mainstream village.

Other Theories of the Origin of Untouchability

Let's us examine the theory of racial differences with the origin of untouchability. According to the theory of Mr. Rice, there are two elements that dominate racism:

a) That the untouchables are non-Aryan, non-Dravidian aboriginals; and

b) That they were conquered and subjugated by the Dravidians.

Mr. Rice opines that India saw two invasions. First it saw the invasion by the Dravidians. Later they defeated the non-Dravidian aboriginals, the ancestors of the Untouchables, and made them Untouchables. The later invasion what India underwent was by the Aryans. When the conflict held between the Aryans and the Dravidians, the Aryans, no doubt, conquered the Dravidians and later made them Shudras. This theory of Mr. Rice is too introspective, mere speculation to expose the thread of the origin of the Shudras and the Untouchables. (Jadhav 2014: 518)

If we examine our ancient Indian history we do find four different races: the Aryans, Dravidians, Dasas, and Nagas. How far it is true we don't know the reality but some Historians state that these four races were not a single homogeneous people but they were divided into two sections having two distinct cultures. One was called Rig Vedic Aryans while the other one the Atharva Vedic Aryans. Their literary texts and opinions also differed from each other. Of course, the Rig Vedic Aryans created Brahmans, Sutras, and Aranyakas. The Atharva Vedic Aryans produced the Upnishads. Some historians also assume that the Aryans were completely a separate race from all other races.

Another confusion lies in the differentiation between the Dasas and the Nagas. The assumption reveals that Dasas are the same as

Nagas. Dasa is a Sanskritised term that originated from the Indo-Iranian word *Dahaka* who was the king of the Nagas. The Aryans subsequently were called the Nagas after the name of their king *Dahaka* which is in Sanskrit form Dasa. So, it was the generic name given to all Nagas.

Another concept of the emergence of untouchability lies in the unclean and filthy occupations of the Untouchables. Evidence declares that Aryans were like any other people of that era and their notion of untouchability did not differ from those of other ancient people. For example, Narada *Smriti* discloses clearly that the Aryans didn't mind at all associating and mixing themselves in filthy occupation. If scavenging was not loathsome to an Aryan how can we say that the same filthy engaged work was the cause of Untouchability? The firm belief in the concept that the filthy occupation brings untouchability to the Untouchables does not seem appropriate.

Dr. Ambedkar in his work *The Untouchables: Who Were they and Why they Become Untouchables* has brought into discussion the major aspects of why the stigma of caste remained stuck only with the Untouchables. There are some major points on that basis a departure took place from Brahmanism to the prevalent practice of untouchability:

a) The Untouchables do not receive the Mantra from a Brahmin
b) The Untouchables are not served by good Brahmins as family priests at all
c) The Untouchables have their own priests reared from themselves
d) The Untouchables eat beef and do not contain reverence to the cow.

The Brahmins didn't like the Broken men simply because the Broken Men ate beef. The issue of the argument of beef-eating created the notion of pure and impure between them. It was beef-eating point that separated Brahmins and the Broken Men. The context justifies those who have a nausea against beef-eating should treat as untouchables to those who eat it. And later they took the support of some Hindu Shastras to ensure the continuation of untouchability. But questions also arise here:

a) Did the Hindus never eat beef?

b) What led the Hindus to give up beef-eating?

c) What led the Brahmins to become vegetarians?

d) Why did beef-eating give rise to untouchability?

e) And when was Untouchability born?

It is impossible to accept the views of learned Brahmins when they hold the notion that they never ate beef and invariably had been vegetarian. Our history and even Rig Veda shows that the Brahmins at one time did kill cows and eat beef unhesitatingly. Every day was a beef-steak day for the Brahmins. For generation after generation, the Brahmins remained beef-eater. The Brahmins not merely were so-called beef-eaters but were also butchers. They also cruelly butchered animals.

But later the Brahmins gave up beef-eating. So, here also question emerges why they gave up beef-beating. What made them take such a new initiative? What was their strategy behind giving up beef-eating? No doubt, it was the conspiracy that made the Brahmins give up eating beef and worshipping the cow. The strategy of worshipping the cow is seen in the struggle between Buddhism and Brahmanism to build supremacy over Buddhism. As we know the strife between Buddhism and Brahmanism which went on for 400 years has been a crucial issue in Indian history and that also left some impressive marks on the religions, politics, and society of India. It's fact that Buddhism at one time had been the vast majority of the population of India. Later, it equally attacked Brahmanism and even reduced the Brahminical hierarchy. Buddhism being dominant defeated Brahmins and so the Brahmins lost all power at that time. Buddhism was all set to establish social as well as political power. After the death of Buddha, his followers started to carve his images place to place and created a space for his worship. But Brahmins who were opponents to Buddhists built their separate temples and designed the idols of their own lords like Rama, Krishna, Vishnu, Shiva, and others.

Why did the Brahmins become vegetarian clearly denotes their strategy? Their strategy was to bring superiority over the Buddhists. It became their compulsion to give up beef-eating. Although the Buddhists were not completely vegetarian yet the Brahmins gave up the notion of beef-eating to replace the Buddhists' honour and respect which they had gained in the minds of the masses by their opposition to the killing of the cow for sacrificial purposes. Even later on, cow-killing was applied socially as a mortal sin by the Gupta

Kings who were the law-makers of Hinduism. When the Brahmins made the cow a sacred animal, the Broken Men still had been eating it that separted them from Brahmins. The Broken Men could not stop eating beef and so it created a sense of 'other' in the eyes of Brahmins. Even when during the period when both parties, the Settled Tribesmen and the Broken Men ate beef there was a difference in eating it; the Settled community ate fresh beef, while the Broken Men had to taste the flavour of the dead cows. There was also a compulsion for the Broken Men not to eat fresh cow because they could not afford it since it was too costly for them. The dead cows became the mark of defilement and pollution for those who avoided it. The flesh of the dead cow became their main source of sustenance. Carrying the dead cow subsequently became an obligation for them that brought stigma of untouchability for them.

The examination reveals that untouchability most probably emerged by 600 AD. Even Manu whose Manusmriti is dated about the second century AD. didn't prohibit the beef-eating or cow-killing as an offence. It is obvious that cow killing became an offence or mortal sin by the Gupta Kings around the 4th century, who were ardent champions of Hinduism. So, it can be said without a doubt that the notion of untouchability came into existence about 400 AD. Untouchability took its birth in the duel between the Brahmins and Buddhism to get supremacy. (Jadhav 2014: 526)

Shambuka's Punishment

The story of Shambuka also refers to criminalising the Hindu caste system and caste atrocities on shudras. When Rama after being a king was ruling Ayodhya, a Brahmin boy died untimely. It was like an earthquake in Ayodhya since the boy belonged to a Brahmin family and no Brahmin could die untimely in Ayodhya as it was Ayodhya people's belief. The dead boy's father came running lamenting on his son's death and wailed before Rama saying that surely there is some great sin in the reign of Rama and the death should be investigated. It struck Rama heavily and he started analysing the cause of the death. After consulting the Brahmin advisers of his area, he came to know that a Shudra was performing tapasya which was against the Brahminical law and order and such violation of rule has caused the Brahmin boy's untimely death. The Brahmins also fomented Rama to take action against that Shudra boy by giving him severe punishment because as a Shudra he had no permission to perform tapasya.

Rama was extremely disappointed at such a frightening incident. He without a delay went out in search of a Shudra to know who is that person that is not sticking to serving the higher Varnas and violating the law to gain Brahminical power. He wanted to know who is that person is practicing tapasya, to give him severe punishment. After a lot of investigation, he found an ascetic performing penance in the northern part of his realm. Rama went near to him and stated: "I am Rama, the son of Dasharatha. Out of curiosity, I ask you this question: tell me truthfully in which caste you have been born"?

Shambuka, the Shudra keeping his eyes down frightening replied truthfully, "O king, I am born of the Shudra caste. I want to attain divinity by such penance". As soon as Rama heard Shambuka's words it extremely infuriated him and without making a delay to ponder over the matter, he drew forth his sword and heartlessly cut off Shambuka's head. Rama felt relieved after the assassination of that Shudra, Shambuka. He realised that Shambuka deserved to be restored to his life and so he had to do it. As soon as Shambuka departed from the world, it was believed that the dead Brahmin boy got his life again; he had been restored to life the moment Shambuka, the Shudra ascetic was assassinated. This reflects the myth of Brahmin's mind-set. This brutal act of Rama exposed the monopoly of Brahmanism in gaining divine knowledge. It was a presage and teaching for all Shudras to learn what happens when a Shudra violates the Brahminical code of gaining divine power – the result is directly assassination as it took place with Shambuka.

Eklavay's Punishment also Refers to a Caste Atrocity

As we know Eklavya was the son of the chief of a forest tribe called 'the nishads' whose main occupation was hunting and fishing. He was a voracious person who was devoted to learning the skills of Kshatriya warfare. So, he found out a well-known archery teacher, Dronacharya. Dronacharya lived in Hastinapur, so, Eklavya set out to meet him. When Dronacharya for the first time met him, he was extremely impressed by Eklavay's sincerity and devotion for learning archery. But after all, he could not help asking Eklavya regarding his caste. It puzzled Eklavya why he was asking about mu caste? But after all Dronacharya was supposed to be his teacher so how could he hide his caste, he had to tell him the truth. So, Eklavya responded to Dronacharya's question, "Sir, I belong to a nishads generation. My father is chief of the tribe and we live in the forests. I belong therefore to no caste, and I long to learn the martial arts".

As soon as Dronacharya heard of Eklavay's caste that he belonged to the nishads generation, he completely denied teaching him pretending that he is a teacher only for Kshatriya princes and not for others. He can't violate the established Brahminical codes by teaching tribesman and so him too. It made Eklavya demoralised and he appeared in a desperate state. Taking back his steps he returned hopelessly to the forest. After introspecting on that issue, he found a way to learn by himself. So, he made a clay bust of his teacher Dronacharya and started practicing archery everyday by targeting that image. Day by day his labour was bringing fruits before him. One day he finally became such a skillful archer. And the day comes when one day he fired arrows into the mouth of a dog only after hearing the sound of its bark. That dog belonged to the princes of Hastinapura.

When the princes and Dronacharya came across the shot of that dog, they started searching for the killer. When they came to know that it was Eklavya, it astonished them that how can he be such a skillful archer. Dronacharya had completely forgotten Eklavya that he ever had visited him to learn archery. So, taking Eklavya unknown, Dronacharya gave him a challenge to a contest. But even in that contest, Eklavya got the victory by proving a skilful archer. Dronacharya asked him who you are. Eklavya replied, he is Eklavya, belongs to the nishads family. Again Dronacharya questioned him who is his teacher? At this Eklavya kept mum for a while and then opened his tongue saying, it was Dronacharya sir. He was surprised to listen to his answer. But I am Dronacharya standing before you and never taught you any archery. But how did you become such a skillful martial man, Dronacharya hesitatingly asked him? Eklavya narrated the entire story of his daily practice through the clay image. He also narrated about his refusal when once he visited him for archery. Now Dronacharya remembered everything still he was not happy since Eklavya was a nishads and a nishads boy didn't deserve to have such a great skill. His archery became famous within a day. But upper caste people never digested it, thinking that can any nishads boy be more skillful than Kshatriya princes? Now Dronacharya found a way to stop Eklavay's archery and unhesitatingly he demanded Eklavay's right thumb as his gurudakshna. Eklavya the honest son of a tribesman without asking more questions cut off his right thumb and handed it quickly over to

Dronacharya. Arjuna was happy that his rival Eklavay's martial art had been destroyed. Immediately Eklavya, a nishad boy became armless. Dronacharya proved that only Kshatriya princes have the right to be archers, tribals don't deserve it and they should continue their own occupation of farming. This manifests Brahmanism's monopoly to push minorities to the outskirts.

Such historical punishments have been recorded in the Shastras evidently to make minorities and shudras aware of the aftermath of the transgression of their assigned jobs. It should be understood clearly that the caste system is merely an ideological system based on hegemony. We should not take caste merely as the barrier of pure and impure but apart from it there is also the opposition between domination and being dominated, ruled and oppressed. Caste system brings unequal access to the same sources as our society monopolises. Depriving depressed class of people from gaining knowledge and arts has been a crucial part of caste system ideology. Such denial has been creating another part of the traditional history of India that remains the crux of inequalities.

CHAPTER 4

Stereotypes of being a Woman

Dalit Women's Movements

To trace the Dalit Women's Movements we must turn back to the twentieth century where some Dalit women fighters and activists have contributed to the development of women emancipation. In the first decade of the twentieth century, we have Shivram Janaba Kamble who was a prominent figure of Dalit Women's Movement. She, very ardently fought against the persisting stigma about the offence of prostitution through the mirror of the Untouchables.

The fight against dalit women suppression takes its beginning from Maharashtra region where several conferences were organised by dalit women. According to the survey, the first girls' school amidst the Untouchable community got started by Kalicharan Nandagavali who subsequently became the first untouchable leading figure from Gondia to the Central provinces Legislative Council. Jaibai Chaudhari was the first woman hailing from Nagpur who founded first the girls' school in 1924, in Nagpur. She was such an outspoken woman who achieved education against the patriarchal wishes of her husband. Along with her, a large group of dalit women came to light to accompany her fight. During the 1930s other groups of social workers gave the foundation of hostels, especially for marginalised girls.

When Dr. Ambedkar founded other *Satyagraha* in 1928, in a great effort to let untouchables allow drawing water from a public pond where dalit women also equally showed their agitation and dare to participate in that battle for fundamental rights. They also equally contributed on the occasions of the subject committee meetings claiming equal rights. When again he campaigned *Satyagraha* movement during 1930 for the rights of untouchable people to have entry into Hindu temples, a vast majority of such community contributed to that movement showing their courage while sitting in agitation in the gate of the temple. This movement went on by 1935.

In the Yeola conference that was held near Nasik, Dr. Ambedkar explicitly announced that his objective was to organise and to awaken the guts of the Untouchables; to make them aware of their deprived rights. The movement channelised the other conference encompassing both men and women, held in 1936 in Bombay in support of Dr. Ambedkar. Fighting woman leaders like Sulochana Dongre of Amravati, Minambai Shivraj from Madras, Shantabai Dani, and several other women willingly supported the movements. The group of dalit outspoken women inevitably joined political campaigns for which some of them got arrested and put behind the bars. The women who once were shy and meek became audacious proving self-reliant.

The courageous dalit women also paid attention to child marriage and the stupid marriage system. It's fact that divorce, remarriage, and widow marriages were already welcomed in the dalit community but these leading figures brought some other reforms in the persisting system of marriage. They actively boosted up the system of widow-marriage, child marriage, and remarriage. They pointed out on why there were some unnecessary rituals in marriage celebrations so they reduced them by boycotting them.

Dr. Ambedkar's main emphasis was on women's empowerment through the ways of education. His movement was all set to educate women, to make them active, to fetch them to the public so that they too like other women could gain respect in the eyes of others. His concern for all women reflects in the promulgation of the Hindu Code Bill where he brought into the discussion about the equal status of women in divorce, marriage, inheritance, and property ownership. His Hindu Code Bill gave a challenge to the boycott of the Law of Manu that aimed to maintain an androcentric world. An organisation established in 1986 by the Bharatiya Mahila Parishad concerned with dalit women's active awareness regarding their deprived rights. The last two pages of that conference entitled "Dalit Women are Slaves of the Slaves" here mentioned:

> Dr. Babasaheb Ambedkar urged us to develop strength and struggle and to give up superstitious customs. He said, 'the appearance of Tulsi leaves around your neck will not relieve you from the clutches of the money lender. Because you sing songs of Rama you will not get concession of rent from landlords. You will not get wages at the end of the mouth because you make pilgrimages every year to Pandharpur. Do not believe in fate, believe in your strength'.

The message here is courageous to enlighten women who stick to superstitious faith and that ultimately bring no change in their desperate life. Dr. Ambedkar wanted to encourage all women that there is nothing like fate; strength and continuous labour can change their life. The context of women's subjugation is also linked between caste and patriarchy and both the weapon are toxic in women empowerment.

In 1942, "The Women's Conference" during the Scheduled Caste Federation meeting held an important event. Ambedkar delivered an enlightening speech, "your dress, your cleanliness and the confidence with whish you behaved in the conference brought delight to my heart" (Ambedkar 1995: 37). Dr. Ambedkar's intention was to awake all the faculties of women so that they could be an inspiration for the next generation of women. His mission was to educate them and so they can educate their children. Women should be conscious regarding bearing children: not to have too many children; and to let equal freedom in marriage, every girl should treat her husband equally as a friend.

After looking at women's marginalised position, Dr. Ambedkar promulgated some laws for their welfare. In 1928, he introduced a bill for working women and enforced a norm of maternity leave for such women. He also supported equal wages for women. Vasant Moon who edited Volume 14 of "Dr. Babasaheb Ambedkar: Writings and Speeches" expressed significant points what Dr. Ambedkar made a speech on the importance of the Hindu Code:

> No law passed by the Indian Legislature in the past or likely to be passed in the future can be compared to it [Hindu Code] in point of its significance. To leave inequality between class and class, between sex and sex, which is the soul of Hindu society, untouched and to go on passing legislation relating to economic problems is to make a farce of our Constitution and to build a palace on a dung heap. This is the significance I attached to the Hindu Code. (Zelliot 2003: 212)

In 1942, two drafts of bills on marriage were presented to be promulgated. Subsequently, a Hindu Succession Bill was introduced in the Assembly. Again in 1943, a Hindu Succession Bill was introduced but referred to a Joint Committee. The purpose of this Bill was to notice that those people who were not Muslims, Parsis, or Christians were included in the Hindu category. Gradually, Dr. Ambedkar perceived that although Hindu Code Bill was introduced in the parliament on 11th April 1947, after four years, it was mercillesly destroyed and unsung. So, the cold soldierly treatment of the parliament compelled him to resign from his post as a Law maker in 1951. The Prime Minister was reluctant to support the demanded Codes. (Rao 2003: 213)

After a long wait, some codes of the Hindu Code Bill were passed bit by bit in 1955 and 1956, not the total Bill. The major provisions among them were to give guarantees of property to daughters from their paternal home; abolition of caste in the matter of marriage and adoption; the principle of divorce; the principle of monogamy. Dr. Ambedkar's mission behind promulgating such Bills was for female equality, recognition of women's worth at international positions. His interpretation over women's right in the field of marriage and property are obvious here:

> I know a great deal of the argument that is always urged against women getting absolute property. It is said that women are imbecile; it is said that they are always subject to the influence of all sorts of people. . . My submission to the House is this. If the woman can be trusted to dispose of her *Stridharma* property (marriage gifts) in the best ways she likes. . . If in certain cases women were competent and intelligent to sell and dispose of their property, they must be held to be competent in respect of the disposal of the other property also. (213)

We can see clearly the women's empowerment in the words of Ambedkar. His motto was also to establish an inter-caste system in the society. He is absolutely right when he says that caste and gender discrimination are the barriers to marginalise enough dalit women. People generally contain their faith in the continuous lineage of family through son; such notion needs to be boycott from family as well as society. He, cultivating the faculties of dalit women, made his views by saying, "It is up to those of us who think best theoretically to more thoroughly explore this issue. It is up to Dalit women themselves to explore ways to control the patriarchy they face both within and without the Dalit family. It is up to all who care about human rights to work for freedom, equality, and justice for women". (216)

We notice in the mission of his Hindu Code Bill the departure of caste and gender-free society. He continuously struggled for the liberation of women. He woke up dalit women of their costume of half-covered sarees, heavy and cheap jewellery are also responsible for the identity of their untouchability. He motivated all dalit women in his long speech delivered at Mahad Satyagraha Parishad, "You all must vow to leave behind the old and the dirty customs. To state the truth there is no branding on the forehead of the untouchable which would mark the caste of a person. I am of the opinion that these customs have in their earlier times been thrust upon us" (Bahishkrut Bharat, 1928). Now the time is all set to throw away all those dirty dresses and cling to a neat and clean appearance so that the public could not isolate them from other women. He came across all the phenomena of the process of women marginalisation and ultimately found that the women's subjugation will automatically come to end the moment patriarchal structures are eliminated. And the development of women is not possible until the caste system is abolished. Mahatma Phule and Ambedkar both raised their finger on the swinging nature of caste and gender discriminated society. They together call upon people to create a non-Brahminical principle-based society.

The Principles of Stridharma

Stridharma is taken as an innate code for women. Society most probably views it as if it is a celestial applicable code for women. In no circumstances women are spared when they transgresses against this code in any caste or religion. When we talk of marginalised or dalit women's stridharma; the Brahminical structures of Hindu stridharma are imposed on them explicitly. The mythical notion significantly discloses that a 'demonic' stridharma was the maternal heritage of women whereas the stridharma or the duty of women was their paternal heritage, given to them through the Brahmin priests. The Brahminical myth says that stridharma was necessary to protect women's sexuality and bring women to the right track from the realm of wild nature. Women's sexuality, their essential female codes, their maternal power had to be controlled through establishing patriarchal weapons to show the world a new social hierarchy.

In the words of Uma Chakravarti, the mechanisms of controls on women were operated through three devices so called three levels: the first level was based upon ideology; the second was the right to discipline and keep women under patriarchal control through the notion of lineage, and the third appeared the imposed punishment by the kings of that time for their errant behaviour. But the crux of stridharma or pativratadharma lies in the training of women in the best possible way. Beginning with Brahminical stridharma, the Hindu religion cultivating such concept also took it necessary, applicable for dalit women. (Chakravarti 2013: 74)

It's fact that any system persists unless or until it is given the opportunity to function properly in the society. Pativrata and stridharma fall under such categories. The upper caste Hindu women considered themselves respective and honoured in their patriarchal family when they stuck with the codes of pativarta and stridharma. They maintained the established pativarta only to gain divine power in the eyes of their men. Any violation against such chastity and honour incurred severe punishment for them. The same superstitious ideology remained the core of dalit women's subjugation when they were asked to follow Brahminical stridharma and pativarta. The actual mechanism and institutionalisation of patriarchy got unmasked when its mission became successful. Patriarchal institutions are structured in this way the certain ideology to be naturalised as God's law.

The story of *agnipariksha* about Rama and Sita also discloses the mask of Brahminical conservative concept for women. The *Ramayana* gives us clear evidence of woman-chastity in a patriarchal structured hierarchy. It is a completely Brahminical text which believes in the stereotype that when a woman worships her husband in the form of God, he becomes her protector and she is so well guarded by him that there is no possibility of losing her chastity and perversion; however, her chastity is supposed to collapse even in the most dangerous situation. Sita, the loving and long-suffering wife of Rama also had to undergo the same ideology of pativarta and stridharma. Rama wanted to examine her chastity through *agnipariksha* to know how far his wife remained chaste in his absence, before accepting her as his wife. Sita had to invoke Agni, the God of Fire, to prove her chastity and pativarta. Agni proved her fidelity by not burning her and so she was declared as a chaste wife. It was only after that *agnipariksha* Rama made his mind to accept Sita as his wife. Then Rama declared that Sita had maintained her fidelity as there was no stain on her character even in her absence and Ravana remained a failure in seducing her.

On the other side, there are also several mythical examples concerning what incurs on a woman when she is suspected in her chastity-examination. Let's have a look at the mythical story of Renuka who was the wife of the sage Jamadangni. Although she was a virtuous woman yet she had to undergo the stereotypical ideology of patriarchy that was only to create a myth to dominate over women's sexuality. She used to mould mud bowels out of wet mud and then she carried water in it for use for her husband. Unfortunately one day she happened to see the image of a passing Gandharva flying overhead and she realised 'How handsome he is?. This feeling was enough to destroy her chastity and it broke her devotion to her husband. And next day when she remained failure in moulding the same bowl and so she could not carry water for her husband that day. When her husband got this change, it startled him too much exasperating him. Her angry husband without making a delay ordered his son Parshuurama to cut off his mother's head. The heartless son also committed the act his father ordered. Since it was a patriarchal society and so every order of the father was welcomed in the family. Had he once thought the love for his mother had given him, he never would have cut off her head. Women are taken as chaste so long as they prove their pativarta theory but once they violate the theory; it is the end of their existence in the world (76). Although how far the mythical examples are true it is very difficult to reach at its right conclusion. But so far as my opinion is concerned I think such mythical stories based on women-chastity are created to subjugate women sexually as well as mentally. Because if the women are examined to prove their pativarta and chastity then why don't men prove their chastity? Every examination is applicable only for women, what a stupid mythical beliefs!

The Stereotypes of 'Saubhagyavati'

Marriage is a social custom where two distinct sexes are united together along with a majority of responsibilities rested upon them. It also ties all the members of two big families together. In the words of a critic Chandra Singh, "Marriage is seen by feminists as a patriarchal weapon that finalizes the complete subversion and social obliteration of woman and although constructed as the apotheosis of fulfilment for both man and woman, it acquires centrality in woman's life only and contains both her space and her identity". (Singh 2007: 49)

Almost in all cultures, a woman is glorified as *saubhagyavati* if she is a married woman and more importantly when she is a husband worshipper. The more a woman bows down before her husband the more she is called a good husband-devoted woman. The entire formulas of marriage are based upon the ideological perception of saubhagyavati. Women in marriage are like a market stock bargaining. She is sold from man to man. Here Levi Strauss' observation is quite appropriate when he, in his work *The Element Structures of Kinship* (1949) argues the value of a woman through marriage tie. He considers the value of a woman as an object of exchange. The bride, the gift, the object of exchange embodies "a sign and a value" through the patriarchal system. A bride functions in a marriage ceremony in her relation between groups of men, she does not possess her own identity. So, through the ritualistic expulsion of women and ritualistic importance of women, patrilineal superiority is secured and patriarchal dominance still remains superior. He emphasises the patriarchal system in a marriage where women in marriage can't claim any identity but only a relational term that both (the bride and groom) tie the various clans to a common patrilineal identity.

This notion of *saubhagyavati* is challenged by feminists who are critical of this term. Mahadevi Verma, another critic rhetorically builds her argument in this context and opines, "Can this buying and selling, this business of marriage be deemed the most sacred bond in the woman's life? Can she become a '*saubhagyavati*', the fortunate one, by having a husband who lacks self-pride the ability to support his wife and is dependent on others?"(Jain 2005: 38). Her observation unfolds the ideological notions of patriarchal institutions. Social structures cultivating the patriarchal threats through the marriage system build new ways for the subjugation of women. Our society never minds to get a girl married out of her will. Even today, in most of the families, parents even don't ponder over whether the groom they have selected for their daughter is able to justify her age, her thinking, her likes, and dislikes. They simply think only two opposite sexes are required to get married. Our Indian culture teaches women to worship their husband whether he deserves that worship or not. It legitimises the ideology that however a husband is stupid or useless a wife has to be a husband-devoted wife. A husband may appear pervert or unfaithful to his wife but a wife should have to be loyal to her husband. "The Indian man picks up a woman to domesticate and rear, just as he picks exotic colourful birds as pets for his pleasure or a cow or horse for his use. He thinks he has the same right over her body and mind as the right he has over his pet birds and animals" (Jain 2005: 233).

She further extends her argument on the animalistic nature of an androcentric world where a woman is nothing but merely a puppet in the hands of men, "Her knowledge, wisdom, talent, and beauty are all merely the means of his self-praise. Whenever this living image of display desires to express her separate individuality and reveals her own distinct inclinations, ideas and opinions, the man unfailingly becomes agitated first and then discontented" (235). The demarcation between males and females encourages violence against women. In a society where human beings are discriminated on a gender basis, there is no space for human development there and in such a trapping world, females fall prone to the constant brutal acts inflicted upon them. If we examine the views of Michael S. Kimmel we get such prevalent creeping ideas:

> In societies in which masculine bravado – the postures of strength and the repression and denial of fear – was a defiling feature of masculinity, violence was likely to be high. It turns out that those societies in which the definitions of masculinity are very highly differentiated. (Kimmel 2008: 317)

In India, endogamous marriage is a persistent norm where marriage is generally fixed within the caste community. They regard 'marriage out of caste' as a big crime, as it transgresses their kinship structures. Almost in every culture, the purpose behind marriage is similar. But the Hindu society is based on two types of marriage: anuloma marriage and pratiloma marriage. When a higher caste man marries a lower caste girl, it falls under anuloma marriage. It is commonly welcomed in Hindu society because a man's seed is obviously regarded as more powerful than a woman's one. And also the Brahminical texts allow such anuloma marriage. On the contrary, when the marriage occurs between a higher caste woman and a lower caste man, it is called pratiloma marriage and such type of marriage is an offence for Hindu upper caste people and that's why they regard it unnatural.

Sexuality and Marriage

Menstruation and baby delivery are the factors that bring notions of impurity to all women in Indian culture. Such type of impurity is temporary and taken as normal. But when it comes to the impurity of dalit women, their impurity of 'untouchability' is innate and it can never be washed away how much they effort to get rid of it, it remains vain. It's true that lower caste men don't perceive so much notion of defilement when their women are in menstruation cycle or delivery process as upper caste men consider their women. On the contrary, in some upper caste families men don't even eat food made by women while having monthly periods, they are not allowed to do religious rituals. But such cultural perception does not prevail as strict rules among dalits. The other feminist critic Aruna Gnanadason also puts her views on dalit women's suppression through marriage and menstruation how the concept regarding women's ritual impurity is associated with their physical constraints, reproductive, menstrual, and sexual functions present them inherently impure. However, these ideas work distinctly for lower caste women because of their vulnerability to control their own sexuality on the interest of the caste. In this way, it is clear that the lower caste men's failure to control their women's sexuality from the claws of upper caste men is partly responsible what makes them impure (Singh 2011: 48). Aruna Gnanadason interprets that ritual impurity and sexuality are the crux of patriarchal authority that plays a vital role in women's subjugation. She further extends her views:

> The idea about women's ritual impurity which arose, along with the physical constraints on their activities, stressed that women's menstrual, reproductive and sexual functions made them inherently impure. These ideas justified her low ritual status within the caste and her inability to control her own sexuality in the interest of the caste. Her sexual insatiability was at the root of all problems. And the lower castes' failure to control their women's sexuality was partly what made them impure. This idea reinforced the caste divisions, and the gender ideology legitimised not only the structure of patriarchy but also the organisation of caste. (Massey 1994: 175)

Leela Dube, a feminist critic makes her points on the hierarchal position of impurity between dalit men and women. She strongly asserts that the dalit men are exempted from doing the impure filthy works like midwifery, washing of dirty clothes, disposal of dirt, and domestic works in upper castes' houses. While their men, no doubt, have also to undertake polluting works like sweeping streets, cleaning gutters, etc. but their impurity is taken into a different context that is sharply different from their women's impurity. On the other hand we find that Brahmin notion of impurity is different. Upper caste women are exempted from such stigma even if they undergo menstruation or child-birth process. Leela Dube castigates explicitly upper caste-based society when she says that dalit women never attain the level of purity of men of their own caste. It is traditionally well known pervasive ideology that dalit women being twice stigmatised.

Widowhood is also a stigma for women. But the set of impurity of widows is quite different from dalit community. A man when he becomes a widower, his manhood still remains as usual as he was having a wife. He is not impinged after his wife dies. But a woman as soon as loses her husband, our society imposes a bunch of codes to lead a different life. She reaches almost at the verge of desolated life. She is asked to put out all the ornaments, colourful bangles, and even she is prohibited from wearing an attractive and fancy sari. But among the dalits such codes are not applicable on widows. A dalit widow leads her life like any other married woman. She is free to do any act she wishes. There are no as such certain rules of restrictions for dalit widows that we invariably find among upper caste widows. Kancha Ilaiah delineates the different notions associating both the caste Upper and Dalit Bahujan:

> When we read in the textbooks that the girls whose husband dies must remain widows and have their heads saved; that they were to be clad only in white, we found it strange. In our families, girls whose in-laws did not look after them well, got divorced very easily and within days second husbands were found for them. While marriages take place at home and are celebrated with one type of meal and drink, divorces also take place with food and drink. Seeking divorce from an irresponsible husband is as much a sanctioned social act as performing marriages. (Ilaiah 2002: 16)

Sexuality and marriage are invariably interlinked to each other. Sexuality is a major factor in marriage in every culture. But the code of sexuality applies differently for men and women everywhere based on virginity. As we see in our society, if a girl loses her virginity before her marriage, she is all the time humiliated by her family as well as a society too much that she reaches almost on the verge of living death. But the same code does not apply to men. Our society never humiliates a boy who loses his virginity before marriage, even if they know about it, it goes unnoticed. Let's examine the impingement of sexuality on gender as well as caste basis. A different set of rules functions in the matter of sexuality and are legitimised for the respective gender and caste as well. We see the involvement of sexuality as a more serious and problematic issue for women than men. And if the issue occurs between two castes and two religions then the case brings dangerous consequences for women. In our country, the punishment of illegal sexuality extremely differs from caste to caste and person to person. The Hindu society considers a woman more polluted and defiled than a man when she makes an extra-marital relationship because they believe that woman is polluted eternally and internally by such sexual acts. While in the case of man, they take it lightly considering transient pollution that could be removed easily.

Leela Dube has rightly made her argument when she brings forth the threads of biased rules of defilement for respective men and women. She says that a woman's defilement through extra-marital affair is like an earthen pot which is easily and permanently defiled but when a man from the same caste or upper caste touches the same defiled women they are polluted for a short term. Our society indeed considers upper caste women deserving severe punishment when she establishes an extra-marital relationship with a man of lower caste. Such women are much more vulnerable in respect of extra intercourse than lower caste women. Pollution incurred through food affects both men and women internally but so far as pollution through sexual intercourse is concerned it is legitimised differently for both the sexes. It should be read through the dictum that sanctions hypergamy although within a well-defined concept, "Superior seed can fall on an inferior field where as inferior seed cannot fall on a superior field". (Rao 2003: 234)

Upper caste men, no doubt, keep mistresses from lower caste as many as they desire for sexual entertainment. When they are caught openly they just perform some formalities to wash that pollution. They take a bath so-called purificatory bath to wash away the impure activity. A large number of Brahmin people in Karnataka and Tamilnadu, discard the old sacred thread and tie a new one along with a purificatory bath after sleeping with lower caste women. On the other side, the system is discriminatory for the women of their own caste if they involve in such an act. If an upper caste woman establishes an extra-marital relationship with a man of lower caste, the same society people severely punish her. She is sometimes beaten brutally, banished from society; even society people perform a 'mock shraddha' (funeral right) declaring that woman as dead.

If we talk of low caste women's sexual exploitation through the hands of dominant upper caste men, we come across many aspects where they are sexually exploited. Normally, low caste women are puppets in the hands of their upper caste landowners. It's fact that the land-lords usually belong to upper caste upon whom women from low caste have to be dependent for their lively. When these women go outside to do field works for earning, the land-lords exploit them in the name of caste and money. Dalit women have some compulsion due to poverty and lack of their own land that makes them to be dependent on the land of the upper caste. The land-lords show their right on dalit women's bodies. They consider a dalit woman's body is a point of attraction and pleasure for all. They claim their open right on their vulnerable body. They persuade such women on extra money more than their earning and then subjugate them in broad daylight. Sometimes we hear the case of dalit women's rape on the pretext of extra payment.

Periyar, the founder of Self Respect Movement tells us about the emergence of the concept of women's chastity. He holds that traditional institutions of marriage which are based on Hindu patriarchal rituals suppress women even today. According to Periyar, when men had successfully established their rights on private property, it led to their desire to have someone to care for their property. So, they aspired for marriage that could give them heirs for their property. Later, the concept of marriage imprisoned women as the protectors of family property. Once they became the guardians of men's property they also became men's private property to produce children as heirs for the family. Subsequently, women lost their right to worship their gods. Instead, the circumstances allowed them to worship their husbands. Chaste wife came to have conventionalised and motherhood an ideal virtue. Women too embraced these roles by presenting themselves chiefly as sexual beings and as mothers. Such practice confined them within the home by bringing ignorance and that prevented their freedom. (Geeta 2015: 101)

> After it had became the norm for people to want children to safeguard property, Brahmins who had invented fictions of heaven and hell to keep the poor from robbing the rich and to amass some of this wealth for themselves now argued that . . . a man must have a [male] child who would keep alive his name after death and perform his yearly obsequies. (Viduthalai 101)

Dalit women are dalits among dalits at social piles due to their caste barriers. They are taken first as dalit women and second as women. Dalit men should pay attention to their women's exploitation. Such men themselves should work hard and stop their women from going to upper caste landlords if they want to protect their women from the jaws of landlords. There is no denying fact that the economic condition is poor in dalit families and therefore dalit men feel forced to allow their women to earn money to satiate their hunger. We see the discrimination even between the dalit men and women on gender factors which cause to succumb to dalit women's identities. A dalit woman is paid less than their men doing for the same job which is really menacing acts. Certain phenomena are accountable to cause early health damage to dalit women. Their early marriage and early pregnancy and also continuous pregnancies break their body which is accountable for losing their confidence. Due to lack of money, they remain bereft of proper health care, and sometimes their suffering body brings premature deaths. Their men also, most often prove to be invulnerable to care for proper medical check-ups to their women.

Rekha Thakur, a social activist, and researcher of Bahujan Mahila Aghadi posits that the Bahujan women encounter exploitation more outside the home than within the family. The mechanisms which relegate such women are mostly established outside the family. They are probably freer within their family than high caste women since the burden of purity and impurity is not on their shoulders. Dalit women have the privilege of separation from their husbands and of remarriage (Rao 2003: 348).

Puberty and Virginity

The cultural set of behaviour structures the foundation of female virginity. Our society brings distinct codes of formulas as soon as a girl reaches at puberty. They are taught to maintain social boundaries that signify the maintenance of their own caste purity. Caste imparts a special code in the mechanism of marriage and virginity. When a girl is born she is brought up teaching womanly characteristics which they are expected to follow in the future. They are instructed what to do and what not to do. And such codes don't stop by marriage but it goes on even after marriage. The mechanism of caste impinges them throughout the life, at every stage of life. Our society remains mum even if they come to know a boy's losing virginity but if a girl loses her virginity and the family members and society come to know of it, they give her severe punishment. She is misbehaved and misinterpreted by people. Even when she is married to someone, her husband tries to investigate her virginity. But the same husband never discloses his losing virginity before his wife. Men forget that if they have the right to have sexual intercourse before marriage, then women too, have the same rights constitutionally. Even if our constitution promulgates equal laws for both the sexes but the problem so far in our country is that the patriarchal mind-set of people doesn't let women go freely. Our society never minds or mocks at a married man who makes sexual relationship besides his wife, they let it go as normal because he is a man. Our society never calls it adultery but if a married woman commits the same act, they take it as an offence just because she is a woman and so she has no right to go against persisting social codes. And such committed adultery of a woman does not get over by the family or society instant but the case is dragged into laws and court where she has to confront humiliation of lawyers and witnesses and others. Such a concept of adultery renders a patriarchal mentality that allows a man to have an extreme right over his wife; it reflects the lord-power of husband adopting his wife as his 'property' to control over her if she makes relationship besides her husband. He reigns over her body as well as her mind. He takes her adultery as a dishonour for him and his family and society as well, but if the same husband enjoys sexuality with so many women then it is not an offence and it does not bring dishonour for his family and society. We can see the biased system of distorted laws codified on women.

Leela Dube asserts that the value attached to virginity is directly linked as a matter of concern with female purity. Society looks pre-pubertal stage of a girl with different eyes. In some castes, when a girl reaches at puberty, a grand celebration is organised to let people know that the girl is ready for fertility. In our country, we see at some places, the custom of worshipping and feeding virgin girls is prevalent even today such as it is seen on the eighth day of Navaratri. This stage embodies the next phase of life. A pre-pubertal girl is looked upon as a manifestation of the incarnation of some Mother Goddess or Devi.

In the south part of our country like Orissa and Maharashtra, we see that a dalit girl's puberty stage is performed with some rituals. They make a separate hut for the menstruating girl which they call 'kuchulu'. The menstruating girl is confined to be there for sixteen days. She takes a bath everyday and is given rice mixed with gingerly oil. Taking bath signifies the removal of pollution. And during such period she is not allowed to do any other outside works. Some women regularly sing surrounding the girl and all this process goes on for the next sixteen days. She is advised by the elder people to hold an iron rod in her hand in order to protect from some evil spirits as the stereotypes suggest them. On the sixteenth day, they burn the 'kuchulu' and the menstruating girl is rubbed turmeric on her entire body and a new dress is clothed. Women surrounding her give her baths one by one and sing some songs. They invite some people and neighbours that day. They come with some gifts to present that girl. They want to spread the news through such rituals that the girl has become a sexual being and thus she needs some protection and vigilance. The girl needs watching over sexual control. Through the rituals they let people know that the girl is ready for marriage negotiation. Of course, a menstruating girl is also taken as untouchable even in upper caste families but their pervasive practice is different. Upper caste people also take a girl's puberty in the context of purity and impurity. It signifies for them to protect the girl's virginity and keep her under scrutiny.

In some parts of our country child marriage is still prevalent. States like Haryana and Rajasthan even today follow the system of child marriage where a baby groom is married to a baby bride. Their intention of doing early marriage is clear; such child marriage ensures that a girl is married with full rites being virgin. But the union of physical touch of both the bride and groom is restricted until they reach at puberty. And in some families, the purpose behind early marriage is something different. There are some poor caste families where parents have to go fileds for their earning leaving their daughters at home. A low caste girl living alone invites many attacks. So looking upon the condition, to secure the virginity and sexual attack of their daughter they get early married.

CHAPTER 5

Dalit Women and Rape

Practice of 'Rape'

The word 'rape' socially is taken as an offence. All types of physical and sexual assaults with women fall under the category of rape. Only a raped soul can feel the severe humiliation and abuse she has to undergo the patriarchal social system. A raped body is most humiliated and insulted in our society although it's not her fault. She becomes an isolated soul who feels completely cut off from society. It is really a disgusting behaviour of our society that hardly expresses anger or disrespect for a rapist but on the contrary, a raped body is easily ostracised from the mainstream society. No boy wants to marry a raped girl. It refers to the honour of a body; it's as if a female's honour resides in her inner parts. And honour is not confined to her body only but even the family, as well as society feel humiliated on her rape. The family, as well as societal honour, resides in women's bodies. But how long we will stick to such orthodox principles, is a kernel point to be noted out. What a shame of such mind-set! If a rapist is not shaming the family and society then why a raped body is viewed as a big shame and dishonour for them?

First of all, it is necessary to look upon its threads that lie at its root. Rape is a social curse which roots lies since the very ancient time. If we look back at the milestones and records of warfare we come across how the practice of rape came to be normalised at the patriarchal set-up. Its root lies in slavery. As human society developed to gain power, it created a space of battle between the master and slave. Historians evidently produce concrete research on the evolution of rape. Centuries ago during warfare, the conquered males were put to death by their captors while females and children of those conquered males were made captive or slaves associated with doing the households of those captors. Looking at the vulnerability and helplessness of those enslaved women the captors misused their body dragging them into illegal sexuality. As there was no alternate except submitting their body before their captors, gave the origin of rape of women. In this way, the process of raping enslaved women by the captors came to establish on the regular basis. (Lerner 1986: 179)

Such enslaved women were being raped brutally everyday and intentionally impregnated, keeping in the mind that once they will procreate children, they wil not escape from their captors' jaw on seeking their children's sustenance. Orlando Patterson interprets how some of the free persons in the ancient time were turned into slaves:

> Slaves were always persons who had been dishonoured in a generalised. . . The slave could have no horror because of the origin of his status, the indignity and all-pervasiveness of his indebtedness, his absence of any independent social existence, but most of all because he was without power except through another. (Lerner 179)

In all circumstances, the captors intended to separate deliberately both husbands and wives so that captors could have thorough command on those women's bodies. The impingement on the conquered of the rape of conquered was only to bring dishonour for women and then by the implication rendered as a symbolic castration of their men. In an androcentric world, a man's masculinity is challenged if they are unable to protect the honour and sexuality of their women. According to Gerda Lerner, the practice of raping the women of a conquered group has been the main feature of warfare from the second millennium B.C. to the present. She asserts clearly that the practice of thrashing slave women as animals and sexual objects by the dominant masters have been prevalent in all periods. The marginalised women like peasants and workers have been expected to serve the sexual pleasure of upper classes whether such women agreed with consent or not it didn't matter for them. During the nineteenth century in Europe, it was common to make intercourse with servant girls by their masters. Later we have clear evidence of using the sexuality of black women by the dominant white males in the United States. Black women were raped by white people due to racial segregation.

If we go back to Mesopotamian civilisation, we get a glance of severe patriarchal society where a man was the sole master of the family. But when that man being a servant of the upper class remained unsuccessful in paying the debt of his master, he had to offer his wife as well as children instead of that debt. The Hebrew Covenant Code (Exod. 21:2-11) also tells us that the male slave must go free after six years of service, leaving his wife and children behind. And even if he desires to stay with his family, he will be consigned to a perpetual slavery. But the coming female debt slave shall not go as free as the male. Once she is freed, she would not be considered eligible for marriage and hence she might be pushed to the job of prostitution. In this way, males in Hebrew slavery had to serve their master for about six years, and then after when it passed on his wife, she might be accepted as a step forward tying through marriage with that master or one step downward master's concubine. A woman's fate would be in the hand of her master for whom she had to serve sexual pleasure. If she appeased her master sexually then her master accepted her through marriage if not, into prostitution.

So, rape has been a social practice that is prevalent in every country or we can say everywhere. No society is free from such disgusting acts. Man through 'penis' subjugates woman, is also a reasonable point. Feminist like Simon de Beauvoir contends that it is biological differences in men and women but the male psychology is something rigid in the light of dominating women. Susan Brown miller views man's ability to rape women as leading to their propensity to rape women and shows how this has resulted in male dominance over women and male supremacy. So, men consider their 'penis' as a powerful weapon to subjugate women by raping them.

In our country rape has become a daily act. Constitutionally the punishment of rape is severe yet several culprits even today after committing rape are roaming free on the road. If we talk of the 2012 rape case of Delhi, it strikes our mind even today. A young girl, Medical student was returning home after watching a movie with her male friend, never had imagined that that night would turn into a nightmare and she will take her last breath. She, with her friend, got into the empty bus. Not knowing the intention of the driver and the conductors, she sat down comfortably with her friend. But as the bus moved a little forward, five conductors along with the driver gang-raped her. Her male friend tried hard to rescue her from their jaws but he remained unsuccessful. They even brutally beat the boy. They mutilated her private parts and even pierced her lifeless body with an iron rod. They assaulted her so harshly that she ultimately reached at the verge of death. Due to fear of the police, they threw her far-flung from the road along with her friend. It was midnight and the road was isolated. After sometime, the police arrived at them and immediately admitted them to a hospital. She was completely unconscious and her every part was bleeding continuously. The boy was also injured violently. But he was saved because he had got minor attacks. But the girl, after vacillating between life and death for three days took her last breath in the hospital. It refers to the violent death of an innocent girl.

After her death, many politicians and known faces commented on her character alleging that she was a girl so she should not have moved outside from home by late-night. Some came up with the contention it was the girl's fault that she was enjoying a movie with her male friend during night hour. Her death was being politicised for a long time. We can see the conservative mind-set of our citizens who allege that girl simply because she had gone to watch a movie with a male-friend during the night show. I don't understand why even educated people contain such menial thoughts regarding girls' moving outside at night. Everyone has right to enjoy his or her life without creating harm to others. We should not take it negatively. We should think that a girl's moving outside doesn't mean she is characterless or moralless, it doesn't mean she is a puppet in the hands of violent people who can attack her sexually. We have to create such a free state where every girl is free to lead her life in her own way. People don't hesitate in alleging a girl who wears short dresses. They explicitly target the cause of her molestation and assault her dress. So, there is an extreme need for change in the mind-set of our citizens. If boys are free to lead their life in their own way, similarly a girl has the right to lead her life freely. If boys and girls are biologically different it does not mean their rights should be different. First of all, it is an urgent need for change in the conservative contentions upon which people generally have been sticking.

If we see the recent rapes in other states we have so many cases. Recently in Haryana in January 2018, six rapes took place within eight days. In Uttar Pradesh also rape is a daily food for violent people. It's not only Haryana and Uttar Pradesh where rape is a persistent practice but it is prevalent more or less in every part of our country. And if we start looking back at all state's incidents we find there are millions of such cases. It is really disgusting when we hear rape of little girls whose biological parts are not even developed. Violent people who are mentally discharged or often voracious of sex can attack any girl whether she is biologically mature or not it does not matter for them, they just want to quench their thirst of sex. Sometimes, we hear of rape committed by the family members of the victim. What can we call such domestic rapes where the culprits are present in the house itself? It is a general concept that people who are drunkards or people concerning low works like rickshaw drivers, auto drivers, or labourers easily prey on women because they are taken low category people who don't care for either their own honour or victims' honour. But what should be called when sometimes rapists are identified as some well-educated and prestigious people about whom society can never even imagine. So, rape is not something that is committed only by the drunkards but it is the mentalilty of people. Rogue people occur everywhere. Not only wearing short dresses, not moving outside till late at night are the cause of rapes. It is all due to violent men's psychology taking females' bodies as a sexual object that appeases them. It is a social curse which can occur anywhere if women are not conscious of their bodies. So, in a way we see, there is gender equality constitutionally but inequalities remain socially.

Rape, molestation, and eve-teasing have been persistent activities in our society. Let's examine Dalit women's rape. Dalit women's rape is taken as normal because our society measures 'body-value' on a caste basis. Upper caste men always stand with on the sexual protection of their own women but they don't hesitate to humiliate dalit women's bodies when they rape them. We hardly hear of upper caste women's rape. And even if it occurs, an instant action is taken into account against the rapist. The rapist is never spared, sometimes put to death by the concerning people of that upper caste raped woman. Law and order also seem discriminatory on hearing of rape issue of upper caste and lower caste women. Court also looks into thorough investigation if the victim comes from upper caste family but on the contrary, the case goes unnoticed if the victim belongs to a lower caste or some other marginalised group because they take lower caste women's rape as minor, not considering it necessary to take any action.

Khairlanji Rape Case

Let's have a look at the atrocities of dominant class people on the marginalised in the city of Mumbai called Khairlanji. At that time Khairlanji was dominated by the OBC people who implicitly supported the BJP party, the Hindu nationalist. The story unfolds in post-Ambedkar reflecting how dalits are forcibly made scapegoats in a dominant powerful society. It is a documentary of a Bhotmange family originally belonged to Ambagad village, which is twenty-five kilometers from Khairlanji. The family comprised Bhaiyalal Bhotmange (55), his wife Surekha Bhotmange (40), their sons: Sudhir (21), Roshan (19), and a daughter Priyanka (17). The poverty crisis made them move to Khairlanji in 1989; a place where Surekha's father-in-law had owned land. But the caste discrimination was obstructing them to grow crops in their own land. Not to argue with the dominant class, this poor Bhotmange family used to draw water during night hour. They had settled in a thatched hut at the outskirts of the mainstream village. They had to encounter brutality of the upper caste people when they somehow after saving money determined to give the foundation of a building. The village panchayat ostracised with the Bhotmange family could not see the development of this marginalised family and began to web treachery to throw them out from the village.

Ignoring the village panchayat's obstruction the Bhotmange family brought the bricks for building construction. Anyhow they built a small house to live in despite the aggressive nature of the village panchayat who was still adamant on the developing steps of dalits as they didn't deserve to lead a modern happy life in their adversaries' eyes. Even though the house was built by God's grace but it remained without an electric connection since they were not allowed to connect wires from the village panchayat. Simultaneously, this dalit family had to confront the hard days in drawing water from the village well.

The wife of Bhaiyalal, Surekha was an outspoken, Ambedkarite spirit, audacious, and intolerant of injustice as she was at least had studied by class nine, that was more than her husband whose schooling was class four. She was extremely a thorough woman who brought up her children with labour and patience. She encouraged her family to utilise the rest of time after farming in rolling bidis – leaf-wrapped and poor man's smoke to earn a livelihood. In this way, their financial income became stable or we can say satisfactory for them. Despite a poor family, it was containing the rays of education, and other privileges like a mobile phone and other things to a satisfactory life that needed in a modern society. Surekha, being a good courageous mother, was trying hard to educate her children to her utmost. Therefore she started resisting her adversaries who were torturing them at every step.

Her first son, Sudhir could not complete schooling after class three as the financial hardship obstructed him to continue it. So, he started co-operating with his family financially through agriculture at his early age. Her second son Roshan was doing his first year of a college course in computers in Mehadi village. The single youngest daughter Priyanka was schooling in class ten, so she was at the final stage of her schooling. Apart from her schooling, she used to associate in extracurricular activities like the National Cadet Corps, the Voluntary military training service for school and college students. Both the sister and brother had to go out of village Khairlanji due to getting education. When Surekha noticed her daughter was having difficulties going on foot at a faraway place for coaching and school, she bought her a bicycle for her convenience. When the neighbouring people came to know of purchasing a new bicycle in a dalit family they could not digest of buying a bicycle for a girl, a kind of resentment, envy and aggression were governing their mind to attack this 'Mahar family'.

It was really a matter of injustice, the dominant class landowners of the village had bounded their own land from all sides and even accused regularly this Bhotmange family by demanding a part of their land to build a road for the village. The village panchayat had been demanding this land since this poor family settled down in the village and occasion verbal altercation had been taking place between them. Several times the adversary Hindu caste people drove their tractors and bullock carts through the Bhotmanges' land damaging the crop in that land. Sometimes they left their animals open to graze the grown crops in that field. Although Surekha's husband who was meek and lenient would let it go unnoticed but not Surekha because she was an intolerant spirit. She continuously kept resisting the atrocities inflicted upon her family and her land.

Now the atrocities were extending day by day. One day, a man named Shivshankar Atilkar, heartlessly loosed his cattle in the Bhotmange field to cause damage to their grown crops. When Surekha resisted him by making some issues with him, he unhesitantly attacked her verbally with vulgar language and even threatened her to murder them, which were enough to know the caste discrimination. She along with her husband went to report the police to take the case into account. Although the police reluctantly registered the report under section 448 (house trespass), section 294 (in causing obscene act at a public place), and section 506 (threat to cause murder) according to Indian Penal Code. They returned home after the case was registered. But the reports remained recorded only in the register and no action was taken by the police because the complaint was against the dominant powerful class, and the reporting people belonged to the dalit community.

When Shivshankar came across the police case reported by the Bhotmange family it infuriated him too much and the next day along with some other village people he gathered around the Bhotmange family, again threatening them to kill the entire family. When the Bhotmange family again went to the police to inform them about the continuous threat, they found that the police had simply forwarded the case to the court without the presence of any witness and so the culprit was discharged. Eventually, the village people, by creating a presence of monopoly forced the Bhotmange family at the end of the tether and became successful in getting a ten-foot-wide passage for the road access. But the police was still mum on taking any active action against the culprits. And the atrocities didn't last here but it created series of violence to root out this dalit family from the village.

One day Bhaiyalal was out of the home to do fieldwork. Suddenly some tractors loaded with the crowd of people drunk including women reached his house and torn demolished his house. Bhaiyalal heard their shouts and running to the crowd he became dumbstruck when he saw suddenly his house demolished from a far distance. A majority of people about sixty and seventy with sticks, chains, and other hard weapons were standing before his house waiting for the family to attack them. Women equally were attacking them. When the duel fight took place, it became public sight. No one was coming forward to save the Bhotmange family. All they were in the favour of village people. Surekha and her daughter Priyanka also became a victim of the massacre. The women also dragged Surekha and Priyanka from the mob, beat them tearing their clothes. Humiliating humanity, they took Priyanka out of the mob to a nearby cattle shed where she was handed over to some violent men. A group of men raped her one by one, to an innocent soul. Surekha also had to encounter such brutal fate through the adversaries. Sudhir and Roshan both the brothers were being lashed out. The adversaries when didn't get appeased, they forced both the brothers Sudhir and Roshan to rape their own mother and sister publicly. The entire family members of Bhotmange appeared helpless vulnerably. The public group kept raping until Priyanka and Surekha took their last breath. Ultimately all the family members of Bhaiyalal passed away in such a disastrous incident. The adversaries then lifted the dead bodies on the bullock carts and dumped them away very far away from the mainstream village. Even though the dead bodies were identified after a few weeks, but no action was taken because the culprits had already shut the door of the police bribing a big amount of money. In this way, we see the brutal action of the dominant patriarchal activities that operate a monopoly with the marginalised people. Had these women belonged to some high-class family, no one could have dared even to touch their body, and the idea of rape would be unimaginable for them. (Teltumbde 2014: 90-101)

Body Matters

Dalit women's body largely matters in the purview of sexuality. They have to carry the double stigma of caste in the context of sexuality whether inside or outside the shelter. Their lowl birth assigns them an autonomous body available for everyone. Here I am examining the same network of dalit woman's body how it operates internally and externally in the sexual context. We can have a look at how a dalit woman's body is assaulted sexually poignantly in Baburao Bagul's well-known story *Mother*. The story revolves around the tormenting life of a beautiful dalit widow who becomes a puppet in the hands of upper caste men. The story is conveyed through the eyes of her son Pandu. Pandu is exasperated when he is taunted by his classmates, neighbouring people, for the supposedly immoral characters of his mother. He also starts calling her a 'whore' when he sees her wearing new clothes, new ornaments, and visiting newcomers into his house. He describes what his eyes grappled one day:

> As he remembered one by one her actions of this morning, a slow fearful suspicion suddenly gripped his heart. It was rue then, perhaps the overseer was her lover. His heart started beating loudly; he no longer felt like eating. To keep himself from worrying about it, he took his school books and slate and sat near the door, reading – his usual practice. But he could not concentrate. The thought of what the children at school would say to him the next day worried him. He thought wildly of running away from the shame and dishonour. He now felt like rolling in the mud, weeping and wailing loudly. (Dangle 1992: 185)

Dangle has depicted a hold on the patriarchal establishment on the body of that widow through the social mechanisms. Pandu the son of that widow equally becomes a victim when neighbouring women hurl abusive words to him associating his mother's immoral behaviour. The beauty of his mother becomes a curse for her. Her husband becomes suspicious of her faithfulness with him. Her husband would have preferred her to be ugly which would not excite others, "His blows were always aimed at destroying her full-blown beauty. He hoped she would lose a lot of blood, become lame or deformed, ugly, and so, despite his ebbing strength, he would aim at her face, her nose, head, eyes" (187). He crosses humane limitations when he tries to brand her with a hot iron to ruin her beauty. She is of course a scapegoat who is sexually exploited by the overseer and also remains under watch of her neighbouring males and females alike. We can see her agony when she cries desperately, "you have all tortured me – you, your father, the men in this street – also the women" (190). A dalit beautiful woman's body is viewed through the threads of sexual behaviour. She is easily trapped in the threads of internal and external patriarchies.

Sharankumar Limbale's *The Outcaste* (2003) that was originally written in Marathi language and later translated into English. Limbale, in this autobiographical book, documents the true events associating with his mother who belonged to an untouchable caste while his biological father was an upper caste who never accepted him as his son simply because an untouchable woman born him who was not his wife but whose father he was. He was born out of inter-caste intercourse. He has minutely manifested whatever society viewed his mother's body. There is no exaggeration in the portrayal of the sexuality of his mother rather he has sketched it out very truly without concealing the hypocritical face of upper caste men how they made his mother sexually vulnerable and how she reached at the end of the tether. The novel revolves around his mother Masamai who treated her as an outcaste son, as a step son. As Limbale himself narrates the encountered strange behavioure given to him by his own mother, "Masamai, my mother, always treated me as if I were her stepson. I was more attached to Santamai, my grandmother. Whenever Masamai began to hit me Santamai would intervene and save me" (42). His grandmother loved him more than his mother. She treated him as his own son.

In the beginning chapter of the novel, Limbale has narrated about his hardship and discriminated life during schooling. "Whenever the school was held in the Marwari's mansion, we Mahar boys had to sit on the floor whereas the other boys sat on a raised platform. We sat amidst the footwear flung all around us. I never touched my teacher's chappals as I was afraid of tainting their sanctity" (05). He also delineates the discrimination how once there was picnic event in his school but the untouchable students were not informed about it so that they could not accompany them for a tour, as their mere touch polluted them. After a few months, he became a serious student in his school and so now the teacher agreed to enroll him in the register. One day, the teacher asked him about his father's name when he noticed his serious interest in schooling. But it was not only a very difficult question but an awkward question for him since he was socially a fatherless child. Since he didn't know who was his father, so how could he let him know his name. So, he remained speechless and puzzled by his teacher's question. The teacher sarcastically called him the 'Patil of Baslegaon'. This epithet was enough to let people know of his birth status and making him the subject of mockery.

As there was no way except adding the name of his biological father, Hanmanta Limbale (the Patil of Baslegaon) before his name, so the teacher was asked to put that name before Sharan's name. When Hanmanta Limbale came across this news, it startled him much and he surprisingly turned up to the headmaster to know why he added his name as the father of Sharankumar. He instantly along with some relatives approached the headmaster to inquire into the matter of his bad reputation. He threatened the headmaster to remove his name from the register otherwise he should be ready to undergo the horrible consequences. He even tried to bribe the headmaster a hundred rupees to shut the mouth but remained unsuccessful since the headmaster was a gentle person who didn't encourage bribes. After much chaos and long argument, the headmaster said loudly, leave it up to his mother, she will tell us honestly who the father of this boy is? Then the mother too approved Hanmanta as her son's father. The novelist kept vulnerably vacillating between caste prejudices.

Once, he had to get the application form signed by his father as well as by the sarpanch. It was a very hard time for him to get the signature of sarpanch. Earlier he used to write his mother's name in the guardian column but now the situation was getting extremely problematic. Day by day his vacillating life was perpetuating into hot water. Hanmanta Limbale, of course, was responsible for wrecking his mother's married life. Her own husband divorced her when he came across the relationship between his wife Masamai and Hanmanta (an upper caste man). Since then divorced Masamai became the keep of Hanmanta. It had been traditionally acknowledged that a big landowner invariably had a Dalit woman as a whore for sexual entertainment. But children born from that landowner have no legal father because the relationship is not legitimate socially. But they blindly made it common practice to have a Dalit woman as a keep. The novelist was horribly watching how his mother had to visit one Patil to another. It was really a troublesome moment for him to cope with the life tumult. It struck his conscience when he saw his mother mortgaging herself to one owner after another. He questioned his own soul, is it a life of a Dalit woman? Is she a woman or some commodity for upper caste landowners?

He along with some other class friends went to the sarpanch to get his signature. The sarpanch signed everyone's application form except him simply because he was subjected as an illegal child. It worried him extremely. The sarpanch being biased towards the prestige of his group people could not see the name of Hanmanta on his form and so denied strongly to return home. The headmaster of the school also appealed to him not to make the student scapegoat but it was of no avail. Even when the novelist put his grandmother's name – 'Santamai Rama Balshankar' yet the sarpanch refused from signing on that name because he was already aware that his grandmother was living with a man, Mahmood, who belonged to the Muslim religion and whom the novelist called Dada. "The sarpanch was in a real fix about how to identify me. But I too was a human being. What else did I have except a human body? But a man is recognised in this world by his religion, caste, or his father. I had neither a father's name, nor any religion, nor a caste. I had no inherited identity at all" (59). Eventually, the sarpanch signed the application by the grace of the headmaster.

As soon as he returned home, he gave a heart-rending cry when he saw his mother. The discrimination and humiliation he was facing out was beyond tolerance and throwing him at the end of the tether. When he turned up school the next day, the class teacher asked him, don't you have a father? It again tormented him. He replied somehow with a suffocating heart, he is dead, sir. The teacher again asked him about his mother. He again felt tormented and humiliated and then replied exasperated, my mother is also dead. When his some familiar classmates saw him replying with aggressive tone, the entire classroom fell silent why he was declaring his mother dead even though she was alive. He states his heartfelt questions:

> I used to ask my mother about my father: What was his name? Where did he live? What did he do? Why didn't he come to me? What was my relationship with kaka? What was relationship between kaka and my mother? Who was Nagi and Nirmi's father? What was my relationship with Nagi and Nirmi? And so on. . . Instead of answering me, my mother clammed up like Kunti. At such moments I felt kinship with Karna. I felt we were brothers. Many times I felt I was Karna myself because, like him, I too was drifting with the flow of the river. My mother asked me to tell my teacher that she was the Patil's whore. This made me very happy and I thought that the next day I would certainly tell my teacher. I didn't know the meaning of the word 'whore'. I thought it meant 'father'. But what a venomous word it is. It implies an impure, foul vagina. Who would willingly enter the gigantic gate of that vagina? (60)

His mother was a village sweeper who everyday got up early in the morning and straight went to clean the village streets. He himself depicts his mother's body portrait, "Her mouth smelt foul and her teeth turned quite black from the herbal powder she used to clean them with" (7). She begged for some left roti or some other food for her children. Whenever a marriage celebration was to be held in the nearby village, they got the opportunity of getting a leftover special food which they could not see at home. So, as usual, once a wedding was held in the village in an upper caste family. Since they were untouchable people so reached there uninvited. They were standing swallowing saliva outside the pandal in the hope of getting some share. They only heard from outside the name of food items discussing among those people. Some invited men were rushing in the raw, some serving others, some were shouting for 'kheer', chapatti, ghee, and curry. While the hunger was making them restless to have it! Ultimately after the invited people went away from the pandal, a servant from the wedding house came to them and asked them to join the feast. As soon as he allowed them, a crowd of entire Maharwada rushed to the feast without a delay. He, along with his sister joined the feast for which he had been waiting since morning. Since his mother never liked to attend such feasts so he had to go with his grandmother Santamai and his sister. As he had no father so he had to follow somebody in the crowd hiding the plate inside the shirt. When after consuming the food there inside the pandal, he tried to carry a little bit kheer for his mother but in the meanwhile a man named Girmallaya snatched his plate full of kheer, throwing the plate on the ground dragged him to mouth shouting in some abusive language like 'son of a bitch'. Therefore, crying loudly he returned home with empty hand.

His mother regularly prepared liquor to sell for survival. Daily visiting customers often arrived during night hours. Sometimes there occurred quarrel between the customers. After drinking liquor some of them even vomited and his mother herself had to clean all the dirt. Sometimes they spit everywhere in the house after taking liquor and his mother annoying cleaned all the spit. Drunkards are not innocent people, they not only sap the liquor but had an evil eye on his mother, Masamai. The novelist as a young boy was watching closely all the evils and misbehaviours of the drunkards. Many a time, he saw the customers gripping his mother's arms when she served them liquor. But what could he do when the business was such a menial. The daily customers harassed his mother fearlessly as if she is an instrument of pleasure. Except that business there was no way out to fetch income for the family.

His family members were also addicted to having liquor because of its easy avail in the house. One day Kamalakka and Nirmi went to the field to get stuff. Kamalakka was a deserted woman by her husband. While Nirmi was about ten years old. Unlike regular, they arrived home until late evening. The entire family was worried about them what happened to them. But fortunately, everything was fine and they reached home staggering as they had drunk too much. Anyhow they lay down on the bed.

The tragedy of a marginalised woman Masamai makes us see how a marginalised husband is also tricked by the land-owner to approach her body easily. Ithal Kamble was Masamai's husband who was employed by the upper caste land owner Hanmanta Limbale on a yearly contract basis. He not only had to work hard in the fields but also in the landlord's house. The novelist depicts Ithal Kamble's physical structures in his own words:

> He was one of the beasts that toiled on the farm. The animals in the shed he looked after were no different from this bonded labourer. Ithal Kamble's poverty was his sad lot, like the yoke-inflamed shoulder of an ox. He worried perpetually about his food. His ribs looked like marks of a whip on the skin of an ox. His stomach was so shrunken that it seemed to suck his back like a lap fly. His life had turned into a cattle shed. How was one to bridle one's tears? How long can one munch on an empty stomach? One had

> to toil like oxen at a plough. The water that sang in the farm-channels carried in it a restless drop of his sweat". (35)

In such a process, Ithal Kamble became the slave of his landlord and was even misused by him. On the one hand, Hanmanta co-operated with this poor family in hardship, and on the other hand he kept his bad intention on Ithal's wife Masamai. He was not hesitating in breaking the poor conjugal life and on the contrary, it gave him pleasure. On the saying of caste council, she had to separate from her husband while her two little children were too young to live without a mother. She became a childless mother after separating from her husband. Now, this poor woman socially became vulnerable. And she was now living in her mother's shelter. After all, every stomach needs food and so was with her. She started gathering wood and sold them in the town for survival. Her husband married again to some other woman. But it was very difficult to remarry for a deserted woman. Our society never respects a divorced dalit woman. And so the novelist narrates this biased kind of privilege given to a man socially, "A man can eat paan and spit as many times as he likes, but the same is not possible for a woman. It is considered wrong if a woman does that. Once her chastity is lost it can never be restored". (36)

Now Masamai an uprooted woman reached at the end of her tether. She was not getting what to do or what not? In such a dilemma she was provided a separate room on rent by Hanmanta Limbale who was responsible for her marriage break-up. He fearlessly was luring her. It became a challenge for her to continue a relationship openly with a man who was responsible enough in her uprooted life. He gradually established full command on her body as now she was a deserted woman. The daily visiting of Hanmanta to her made her pregnant. She didn't miscarriage the baby and gave birth to a healthy baby boy. But now what the question strikes us, who was going to be called the father of that illegal son? The child now became the naked proof of Hanmanta's sexual relationship with Masamai. He never wanted this child to come into this world but Masamai didn't let it happen. The novelist himself narrates about his birth:

> After my birth the mansions of the Patil community must have become tense. My first breath must have threatened the morality of the world. With my first cry at birth, milk must have splashed from the breast of every Kunti. Why did my mother say to the rape which brought me into the world? Why did she put up with the fruit of this illegitimate intercourse for nine months and nine days and allow me to grow in the

> foetus? Why did she allow this bitter embryo to grow? How many eyes must have humiliated her because they considered her a whore? Did anyone distribute sweets to celebrate my birth? Did anyone admire me affectionately? Did anyone celebrate my naming ceremony? Which family would claim me as its descendent? Whose son am I, really? (37)

After his birth, Hanmanta who was his biological father started ignoring him. He never acknowledged as his offspring because it was below his dignity if he cared for him. The novelist is greatly upset by the social prejudices which never value a dalit woman's body. Masamai's tragedy brings forth how a beautiful dalit body becomes the object of entertainment for upper caste people. To be a beautiful woman is really a curse in a caste-ridden society. It renders a different psychological effect in a patriarchal society. Masamai was a beautiful woman and so she had to encounter patriarchal threats in her entire life. What can we call such a relationship when a landlord destroys a woman's conjugal life? And when she is deserted, she just becomes the puppet in his hand who after enjoying sex, deserts her into quicksand. Her tragic story compels us to see how long a deserted marginalised woman would go on without a man? She is transferred one after another powerful man. Now she remains at the mercy of others waiting for bread for her children. Masamai once the keep of Hanmanta later became someone's keep.

The novelist also narrates the other incident regarding his grandmother Santamai. She used to borrow some money from other people, sometimes for the convenience of her grandson. As usual, once she along with the novelist turned up to a money lender. The money lender was in full drunk and was staring at the peeping breast of Santamai's torn blouse. It infuriated the novelist extremely. In the words of the novelist, "His look spread like poison in my heart. I wished that the blouse of this moneylender's mother or sister was torn so that I could stare at their breasts. I burned within. Our poverty was detestable. I wanted to rebel against such humiliation" (82). Whoever his mother and grandmother went to, they shamelessly threw evil eyes on them. Everywhere they were looked at as wild animals. He is cursing God in his own painful words:

> God discriminates between man and man. He makes one man rich and the other poor. One is high caste, the other untouchable. What king of God is this that makes human beings hate each other? We are all supposed to be the children of God then why are we considered untouchable? We don't approve of this God, not this religion, nor this country because they ostracise us. Why are we ostracised? Why are we kept away from other human beings? Why are we kept out of our own selves? Why this

> discrimination between one human being and another? After all, isn't everybody's blood red? (62)

Baby Kamble's autobiographical novel *The Prison We Broke* documents the perpetuating internal and external patriarchies. This realistic novel reveals the certain cultural practices and women's subjugation before these Mahars converted to Buddhism. Kamble, in this novel, speaks specifically about 'Mahar' caste dalit women and their predicament both inside the home and outside the work place. She brings forth the stereotypical superstitions prevailing among Mahar caste, a noticeable culture, and practices different from the Hindu Brahminical culture. She tells us a different set of the upbringing of children among her caste. She strikes our conscience when she discloses her own tragedy when she was a very young baby. When she was only one and half years old and unfortunately falls ill, her family, as well as the surrounding people, assumed her dead, and then simultaneously they started preparing for her burial. The novelist's mother begs to hold her child in her lap:

> When they had dug enough, my chulat aaja bent down to pick me up from my aai's lap. But she clung to me fiercely and would not let go. There was a sort of tug of war for a while. Then, with tears pouring down her eyes, she begged people around to let her hold her child in her lap at least for the night. You buried all my daughters in the night. Now let me at least hold this girl in my arms till the break of the day. Let me gaze at her face, I won't see it again. (Kamble 2009: 02)

The narrator portrays her father's patriarchal violent nature who often beat his wife. Her innocent mother was opposite to her husband, appeared self-centered, and never approved of her husband's patriarchal domination. She declared both father and mother narrow-minded people who most of the time stuck to the old beliefs. She writes about her own mother's imprisoned life in a pathetic tone, "My father had locked up my aai in his house, like a bird in a cage. Whatever money he earned, he would squander away. While his contracts lasted, there would be plenty of food, clothes, and fun. But when he was out of work, we had to go without food even" (Kamble 2009: 05). Her encounters as a dalit woman gave her a close insight into the plight of dalit women. The narrator realistically depicts her familial gender discrimination pervasive to the extreme account:

> The honour enjoyed by a family was in proportion to the restrictions imposed on the women of the house. When no one could see even a nail of the woman thus confined within the four walls of the house, then this

> honour became the talk of the town – a byword among the relatives and friends in the surrounding village. The people would tell each other, how one Pandharinath Mistry kept his wife completely hidden in the house and how even the rays of the sun did not know her. (05)

The novel is the true depiction of a world where dalit women themselves are more active and autonomous in performing inside and outside daily activities. They clean their house, cook food, wash clothes, care for children and on the top of those works they go to filed for farming to co-operate their men. The narrator is extremely troubled by examining the dalit women's hard labour, via their household chores, the filth and squalor, and their nonexistent position. She has brought into light the impoverished projection of their house-utensils how tattered and broken their pots are! "A clay pot would have at least two or three holes, large enough to allow entry to at least a couple of mice. They would close the holes with ragballs, which had sharp babhul thorns stuffed inside. This would prevent the mice from chewing them away. The delicately engraved mouths of the clay pots were usually broken and the pots chipped and cracked". (170)

The novel is laden with rituals and ceremonies examined minutely by the narrator itself. All the rituals are largely performed by the women itself. Even when the matter comes of possession of peys and ghosts, the collective majority consider even peys as female gender. The narrator harshly attacks the stereotypical Hindu belief concerning such orthodoxical ideologies and makes her argument in details by boycotting it. According to her, such a Hindu mindset is nothing but the patriarchal power on the control of dalit women's bodies. We can have some explanations here in the narrator's words:

> Hindu philosophy had discarded us as dirt and thrown us into their garbage pits, on the outskirts of the village. We lived in the filthiest conditions possible. Yet Hindu rites and rituals were dearest to our hearts. For our poor, helpless women, the haldi-kumkum in their tiny boxes was more important than even a mine full of jewels. (18)

The narrator further extends her overviews of the alienated status of daughter-in-law in her in-laws' house. It is really shocking when she reflects the sustaining patriarchal authority generation after generation. The elder women of the family inevitably following the previous patriarchal activities apply to their own younger daughters as well as daughters-in-law. Of course, women's place is assigned secondary in a patriarchal family but what is more poignant to notice here is that even in such hierarchies, women hierarchies prevail. A daughter-in-law is dominated by the male members of her family as well as by her mother-in-law who is herself a woman. The narrator brings to light how in a dalit patriarchal family, a dalit daughter-in-law is mistreated and alienated all the time. She becomes the subject of torture. Even after cooking food, she can't eat first because according to them, it is the transgression of the system. She has to wait for long hours for her male members' eating and then mother-in-law's eating is over; then she could consume whatever the left food is in the pot:

> The daughters-in-law, worried whether any food would be left for them at all, stared anxiously at the quickly depleting mixture on the plate. Since they were daughters-in-law, decorum demanded that they eat only after the children had finished. The poor souls could do nothing but just stare at the plate, licking their lips, hoping against hope that some food remained for them. Just in case a sasu noticed this, she would contemptuously throw a morsel at her daughter-in-law, saying, 'push that down your throat, you shameless hussy! Aren't you ashamed to stare so at a child who's eating? At least let the food get down his throat? Your evil eye will make the child choke. (30)

It is obvious from the text to observe what the lowest position is imposed on a daughter-in-law in a patriarchal family. She is treated no more than an animal. Even an animal is sometimes treated lovingly but not these daughters-in-law. A mother-in-law holds all the power before her daughter-in-law. She often hurls abuse thundering over daughter-in-law even before the neighbours, where sometimes the neighbouring people come quickly to see the violent scene occurring between them. The narrator is really appalled by looking at the tortures tortured by the mother-in-law in the family. A daughter-in-law, daily, has to rise reluctantly about three o'clock early in the morning even when there is no sound of birds and crows, for fetching water, grinding, and other activities for the morning household chores. The mother-in-law is always worried to not let her son blindly fall in love with his wife. She never lets a moment go without criticising his wife before him to separate them. So, the daughter-in-law more often lives under constant fear, like a lamb. When her husband instigated by his mother beats his wife, the wife has to tolerate all such humiliation and lashing out of her husband like a dumb. She becomes the victim of male violence. Sometimes the father-in-law too joins the husband in his daughter-in-law's beating. It exposes the cruel face of male violence displaying the authority of men who are born with such rights of beating women. They feel proud of their virility when they lash out their women.

"Husbands, flogging their wives as if they were beasts, would do so until the sticks broke with the effort. The heads of these women would break open, their backbones would be crushed, and some would collapse unconscious. But there was nobody to care them" (98). Baby Kamble's principles on feminism really convulse our conscience abundantly. She has attacked all the threads of suppression, tortures, and humiliation of a dalit woman in an androcentric world how when a brutally beaten woman goes to take refuge to her natal home, there also she has to undergo again some tortures. There also she has to tolerate beatings of her own brother and father who equally torment her time and again. Again she returns to her husband's home where her in-laws had been waiting for her to teach her some lesson. So, in a way, a dalit woman's life is really painful and pathetic. Sometimes such an escaped woman has to confront the physical assault by her own in-laws and so she lives under fear of losing prestige. The narrator is extremely pained on the inciting act of a mother-in-law who wife by shedding crocodile tears provokes her son against his wife reminding him of his virility:

> You are a man. You must behave like one! You must be proud and firm. You must walk tall. Twirl your moustache and show us that you are a man. Are you wearing bangles like a woman? Then? Do you know about that Aaja of yours? [. . .] Once his wife smiled at his cousin. Finished! He lured her with sweet words, took her to a field, and just axed her down. Cut her into pieces there and then! [. . .] You must chop off your wife's nose and present it to her brother and father. They mustn't have any respect left to sit with the members of the panch'. (100)

So, it is not only men who suppress women but the hierarchal women positions also reduce them to the fringe of the subject of sexual, mental, and physical attack. Elder women too, are partly responsible for contributing to the pervasive patriarchal systems. Their inciting act to a man against his wife is the major point that should be taken into account for consideration. The narrator shows her concern for dalit women's thwarted position. She herself had been afraid of her husband when she was almost on the verge of getting this autobiographical book to be published. She remained scared thinking that, "he would not have tolerated the idea that I had taken to writing. I used to be scared of him" (147). This challenging statement brings to light the patriarchal mind of men who don't spare their women when their male ego is hurt. She also tells us how once when she was travelling by train along with her husband, some men sitting on the train were staring at her. At such an act her husband started lashing her out violently publicly, even without her fault. She was like a slave in his hand. He used to beat her whenever he desired. Her fate was determined through his will. As here she articulates, "He would beat me up for some flimsy reason. Actually, he used to be very suspicious. I tried very hard to prove my innocence. I used to cry, explain, and plead with him. Then for a few days, everything would be normal" (155). Like Bama, a dalit female writer, Baby Kamble also asserts dalit men's frustration and humiliation by the upper caste men as the major cause of suppressing their own dalit women. In her words, "Their male ego gave them some sense of identity, 'I am a man, I am superior to women, I am somebody. If the whole village tortures us, we will torture our women'" (157).

Meena Kandasamy, a dalit activist, leading figure, poet, and novelist voices out the concern regarding 'gender inequality' and 'sexual politics through her literary genres. She also asserts strongly that dalit women are not just victims of the lust of the dominant upper caste men but their continuous fighting against the injustice perpetrated against them comparatively upper caste women, has also marginalised them through all ways. In her poem "Songs of Summer" taken from the anthology *Touch*, she explicitly attacks male behaviours that circumscribe dalit women:

> To make her yours and yours alone,
> You pushed her deeper into harems
> Where she could see the sunlight
> Only from the lattice windows.
> Domesticated into drudgery she was just
> Another territory, worn out by wars. A slave
> Who maintained your numbers. (Kandasamy 2006: 112)

Kandasamy as a poet decries the society that doesn't value women and respect their status. She poignantly condemns the discriminatory society that never values a woman's aspiring features. She contends that when a girl is married she is measured on the ground of education, beauty, virginity, her politeness, and submissive nature but can a society measure a groom on such grounds? She presents such a situation in the following lines of the same text:

> Your society always makes
> The spoon-feeding – the man
> The pot – and pan banging.
> The sweeping-the – floor
> The masochist slave
> And other submissiomen
> As goddess. (130)

CHAPTER 6

Dalit Women in Polygamy

According to Engels, in the ancient time, men and women were free to have sexual intercourse with whom they desired. There was no as such sexual taboo those days. Women were more dominant at that time. But with the emergence of production man owned women as private property and even began to control woman's sexuality. Therefore, free sexual love to women lost its position but it still remained to continue to men. Further, a woman was bound to a single man and she could only belong to that man; except that man, her sexual intercourse with some other person began to be called illegitimate relationship and thus called to bring the family members and society into disrespect. In this way, monogamous marriage became the main norm of the society which was implemented only for women, not to men. It was economic production that enhanced the familial and social power for men over the sexual authority of women. A conventional code was established into practice that a man can marry as many times as he wished but it was against social norm if a woman wished more than one husband. This established code of patriarchal structures which allowed men to have as many mistresses and wives as they wanted but women on the other hand had been loyal and chaste to the ideal of polygamy. Capitalism enhanced the sexual and physical abuse of women by men continuously. (Engels 1983: 73)

Sharmila Rege, in her compiling work *Writing Caste Writing Gender,* a narrative of dalit women, has explained the curse of caste and the polygamous practice of dalit family. In her chapter "Shantabai Dhanaji Dani" (1919-2001), Rege, explicitly brought to light the polygamous nature of dalit family while pinpointing the polygamous family of Shantabai. Shantabai, who hails from Nasik, remained one of the active leading figures of Maharashtra State Legislative Assembly from 1968 to 1974. Later in 1964, she actively took participation in the Satyagraha of the landless launched by

Karamveer Dadasaheb Gaikwad. There she worked as the secretary of the Ramabai Ambedkar hostel. Her welfare in the field of society associating with the marginalised people especially for women empowerment is obvious in her contribution to the foundation of the Dr. Babasaheb Ambedkar Dynan Kendra, Kunal Primary School, and Ramabai Ambedkar Kanya Vidyalaya in Nasik. Shantabai's father domesticated buffaloes in order to gain earnings for the family living. Her father also was addicted to having liquor. Subsequently, he started shirking his daily job and most of the time sat leisurely at home. While her mother worked hard the entire day in the field.

Shantabai unfolds the pitfalls of polygamy in her family. She dictates, her father married twice and had two wives. Her mother was much laborious and toiling throughout the day. Despite her mother's following familial conventionality, her father was more fascinated towards his new wife. His attention was more on his new wife. He ruled over the entire family and his words were must be followed by the entire family members. But he was neither interested to earn money nor looking after the family at all. Contradictorily, he had close eyes on her mother's earning and even doggedly beat her up frequently. Whatever money she earned by shedding her sweats, from sunrise to sunset, he tried to snatch them from her, expressing his manly command over a wife. In this way, his philandering habit had fettered her. Shantabai's eyes were watching all these social freedoms of a man in her family. All this polygamous oppression of her father was choking her mother while the new mother remained unstressed only because of the prestigious position assigned by her father. The observations clarify that polygamy appears a dire menace in many ways for all women whether it is Dalit, the Black marginalised, or any other woman. Its consequences take a woman towards a hellish life.

P. Sivakami's masterpiece *The Grip of the Change* (2006) is a semi-autobiographical novel where she has brought into light the undergone victimised atrocities by upper caste men as well as dalit men. It reflects the monopoly of a polygamous society where this dalit woman appears puppet in the hands of men. The novel revolves around a dalit widow, Thangum, whom the patriarchal system crushes through all ways. She is a woman of nowhere. She is a dalit widow whose husband leaves the world in his early stage of life. After the death of her husband, she became the victim of sexual attacks at the hands of her in-laws. She hurriedly arrives at Kathamuthu, the village dalit panchayat, carrying her complaints. On asked by Kathamuthu, she narrated, "Ayyo. . .Ayyo. . .They have butchered me. . .Ayyo. . . The figure cried like a wounded animal and finally fell down" (Sivakami 2006: 03). Kathamuthu patiently was hearing her painful story but in the meanwhile his own two wives interrupted their communication, asking the widow why she was roaming early in the morning. Thangum, the widow broke her silence, "What can I say? May they be hanged! May they go to hell! The ground will open up and swallow you. You will eat mud. Bastards! You abused a helpless woman. You curs!" (04). Kathamuthu, not being aware of her miseries, curiously wanted to know exactly what incident took place with her. When his eyes watched her abusing her own concerning people in foul language, it incited his anger and he himself shouting at her reflected manly position, "Shut up, bitch! Don't you dare use foul language here? I'll hit your mouth. Don't you have any respect for the man you're talking to? If you've nothing more to say, piss off!" (04). She kept sobbing and heaving sighing and subsequently lifted her wrapped sari and then unveiled her injured part. The dried bloods were stuck with her back parts. She was crying helplessly. She told Kathamuthu (whom she calls Sami), "Sami, these hooligans who beat me up, they should be jailed for at least a day and tortured. The pain is killing me". (05)

The difficult circumstances and economic burden of her livelihood compel her to work in the field of upper caste owner Udayar. So, she started living separately from her in-laws and began earning herself. Now, her body becomes an instrument of pleasure for her field owner Udayar. She becomes a victim of exploitation between internal and external patriarchies. What could a woman like Thangum do who neither belonged to her home nor world? Udayar begins to sexually exploit her in lieu of money. Her family people created the rumour of the sexual relation with Udayar. As she states before Kathamuthu:

> My husband's relatives spread the story that I had become Paranjothi's concubine. That's why Paranjothi's wife's brothers and her brother-in-law, four men, entered my house last night. They pulled me by my hair and dragged me out to the street. They hit me, and flogged me with a stick stout as a hand. They nearly killed me. No one in the village, none of my relatives, came to help me. I begged for mercy, but they would not stop. They abused me and threatened to kill me if I stayed in that village any longer. They called me a whore. (06)

She was wailing before Kathamuthu and narrating all the mishappening. Udayar was making intercourse with her separately in the field where no one probably could notice his sexual perversion. She further extends her tortures:

> Sami, is there anywhere on earth where this doesn't happen? I didn't want it. But Udayar took no notice of me. He raped me when I was working in his sugarcane field. I remained silent, after all, he is my paymaster. He measures my rice. If you think I am like that, that I am easy, please ask around in the village. After my husband's death, can anybody say that they had seen me in the company of anyone? My husband's brothers tried to force me, but I never gave in. They wouldn't give me my husband's land, but wanted me to be a whore for them! I wouldn't give in. Each time one of them came near me I brandished the broom. After that none of them came anywhere near to me. I am a childless widow. There is no protection for me. (07)

She disclosed before Kathamuthu, Udayar everyday raped her in the motor-shed. She no longer could resist that as there was no alternate before her. Every time he raped her and provided her twenty-five or thirty rupees as compensation. On the top of it, he asked her shamelessly to avail more women from 'cheri'. One day Kamalam's brother caught Udayar and Thangum naked together and so instantly he spread this news to his sister, wife of Udayar. When their sexual relationship comes into the public eye, Udayar instead blames Thangum. He makes it a point to project his own image as that of a pure and innocent person. But his hypocritical nature exposes the true picture of Brahminical patriarchy when he contradictorily shouts publicly at Thangum in abusive words, "Ungrateful whore! Even if she was hurt by the hand adorned with gold! A Parachi could have never dreamt of being touched by a man like me! My touch was a boon granted for penance performed in her earlier births! And then the dirty bitch betrays me!"(31). Thangum is brutally assaulted by the relatives of Udayar but none come up to protest against such an act of injustice.

This novel is the best example of dalit polygamy and can be observed through a patriarchal lens wherein the novelist has talked of the persisting nature of polygamous society. Kathamuthu itself is a product of a polygamous society who had possessed two wives. He completely had governed the living life of his two wives. Even the eatable items were cooked on the choice of Kathamuthu. Whenever his wives tried to open their tongues before their husbands to bring something special for cooking, he rebuked them instantly in abusive words. His first wife, Kangavalli, was a victim of patriarchal society who could not have any control over her husband's second marriage. His second wife, Nagamani, was a widow who was struggling with a hard time in her life and who got refuge in Kathamuthu's family by marrying him. Kathamuthu's both the wives work like a parasite who can't even speak without their husband's allowance. He, from time to time, warned his wives not to speak equally with him because being women they didn't possess equal rights to bellow at their husband. In the beginning, both his wives used to comply with whatever he ordered them. His words worked as manly, and authorial command for them. They pressed his legs and served him time to time but the scenario got changed as soon as his interest roused in Thangum, a victimised widow, who approached him begging for some help.

She approached Kathamuthu for a clue but he too committed the same social mechanism. Although he provided shelter to this refugee widow, it created a familial clash in his own family. Both the wives of Kathamuthu became suspicious of his philandering nature. Now even after Kathamuthu's calling twice or thrice, his wives neither came to him nor did they even care about his words. His philandering attitudes towards Thangum compel both the wives not to show any affection towards him. At the ignoring attitudes of his wives, he began to treat them violently, bellowing, if they don't care about his commands he will have to possess another wife. So, here the 'another wife' he was referring to was none other but Thangum. Here, Kathamuthu conveys the pervasive aftermath of dalit polygamous marriage. This reflects the hypocrisy of the Hindu caste system that on one side allows people to hate the lower caste women labelling them untouchables while on the other hand their sexual lust gets fulfilled through these dalit women. Their notion of defilement and purification vanishes when they establish sexual intercourse with such women. The upper caste men like Udayar, link the body of dalit women to their livelihood. It can be clearly seen that Udayar uses Thangum's body simply because she was a vulnerable woman, had to work in his fields for her livelihood. This woman, who is barred from entering her house, goes to the dalit Panchayat leader Kathamuthu.

Kathamuthu was guiding Thangum in lodging the rape case against Udayar. But instead of that help he too was robbing her implicitly. He instructed her how to beg before the inspectors in the police station. So, everything went accordingly. The next day he led her to the police station. She posed there the way Kathamuthu had instructed her. As she saw she fell on the inspector's feet and started wailing about her rape exploitation. But the inspector didn't like her falling on his feet and so instantly he took his feet back asking her to calm down. Then he registered all what she narrated to him. Kathamuthu himself demystified the propositions before the inspector saying Thangum belongs to a lower caste family and so her landowner exploited her sexually. Could he have committed such a heinous crime with a woman belonging to his own caste? A dalit woman's body is a sex symbol that's why they drag their body. In this way after complaining, they returned home instantly. After a few days, she heard people quibbling, "They beat him up. Good! Why did they leave her alive? That whore thinks too much of herself. She thinks that she is very beautiful. That's why she went after that Udayar. When she loses her shape, he will throw her out, and she'll be in a state worse than a dog's". (28)

When the next day police reached Udayar's house during the evening hour, he persuaded the police using his power of money. He hosted the police in a very impressive way, joined them on tea, and also fed them some sweets. He kept alluring the policemen by feeding them plenty of sweets until they agreed to bury the case. He shut their mouth bribing with a big amount since he belonged to an aristocratic family. Immediately, the police handed him over a paper where the case was changed from sexual to caste abuse. It delighted Udayar and he heaved a sigh of relief. He had even won the police. The police then ordered Udayar to pay two thousand rupees cash to Thangum for her compensation, and the rest of the issue police will solve. And so did Udayar. Next day when Ramalinga Reddiyar enquired Udayar to know exactly why the police visited him yesterday? Even before Reddiyar, Udayar saved himself, and alleging thorough Thangum saying, "The Paraiya bitch who was working for me had misbehaved, so my men punished her. She went to Athur and took Kathamuthu's help to register a police complaint". At this Reddiyar incited him, making derogatory on Thangum, "you should have hacked her to pieces and buried her" (49).

Thangum now whenever remembered Udayar's sexual use of her body, she felt hatred towards it. She living in Kathamuthu's family had become part of his family. Kathamuthu's both the wives sat together in the courtyard with Thangum. Kathamuthu took all the ten thousand money which Thangum had won the case. He now entertained everyday delicious food on her money. They gave her food, and so now every Sunday meat lunches had enhanced her glow on her face. Kathamuthu bought her polyester saris as she had only tattered clothes. Kathamuthu's patriarchal inherent thoughts reflect in his attitudes when he shrieks at his wife when she asks him to get meat from market. One day he asked his second wife, Subramani, to hand him a bag in order to get nutrients from the market. Subramani quickly handed him over a bag. Then asking by Kathamuthu, she listed him so many things like onion, garlic, tomato, and meat. As soon as Kathamuthu heard her say 'mutton' it angered him. And retorted her, "Oh, yes, why not? Your father left ten thousand rupees with me. With that money, you can eat mutton every day. Some good lady has given us money that you are all enjoying" (89). Thangum felt exalted when she heard the word 'good lady' from Kathamuthu's tongue. After all, it was her money which they were squandering.

Thangum was happy to get honour in Kathamuthu's eyes. He was giving her some privileges comparatively to both his wives. Before going to market he made his mind to have some liquor. So he asked his first wife, Nagamani, to get four glasses and gives the brandy to Thangum. While his wife resisted over it, Kathamuthu reminded them, it is this widow's money that they are able to have a flavour of some foreign liquor otherwise had they even imagined for it? Since Thangum was not habitual of having liquor so it fouled her, she didn't like even its smell. When Kathamuthu persuaded her she drank it in a breath closing her eyes. That night, every one ate mutton and drank bellyful. But today Kathamuthu's lust towards Thangum gets extended. When the entire family is calm, all went to their own bed. He said both his wives, why they don't go to sleep in the next room under the fan? Both his wives became surprised to see him in his love showering at them today. Both the wives ignored him and deliberately stayed in the same room. They kept an eye on him pretending as if in full sleep. Kathamuthu stood up and bolted the door from outside. Then he turned his eyes towards his daughter's room where she was lying closing her eyes and books dispersed. She was yet awake. Kathamuthu also bolted her door from outside. He was extremely intoxicated by the alcohol. Now day by day his attraction towards Thangum had infatuated him. It was nearly midnight and poor Thangum was lying in the kitchen alone. He instantly went to her to have physical pleasure. Showering his love on her, he remarked, "Why don't you eat something"? When she didn't answer him, "he smoothed her hair and snaked his palms through her armpits, and pressed her breasts. She turned over and he fell over on her". (93)

Kathamuthu's allurement towards Thangum marks that he wanted Thangum to be possessed by him as his third wife. But Thangum protested him by uttering in a very harsh tone, "You are like a brother to me...a brother..." (93). Then embarrassed Kathamuthu left her asking her to adjust her sari. He instantly heard his daughter Gowri's door rattling, so he unbolted her door. Feeling embarrassed he asked her if she was yet awake? Without making a word, Gowri straight turned to the kitchen form where a voice pierced her ears. She saw Thangum was still awake. Her eyes were half shut. She perceived everything that the hellish occurred in her family. She was suspicious of her father's patriarchal domination. She knew it was her father who wanted to have pleasure from this widow. Gowri without a delay speaks loudly, "Dogs! Dogs in this house! Shameless as dogs!" (93). Gowri, as a young girl, was exasperated by her father's patriarchal and immoral nature. As a school-going girl, she knew the ethical values of a person. Through the character, Kathamuthu, Sivakami, has emphasised the dalit polygamy where all women are chained through this lethal practice.

Another incident regarding polygamy can be seen at another place in the novel. Sivakami narrates the consequences of patriarchal threads in portraying a dalit woman's tragedy of Kannamma's daughter-in-law. Kannamma's daughter-in-law loses her life by committing suicide due to the stigma alleged by her husband. Her husband was a liquor addict who brutally lashed his wife often. He sometimes alleged her whore. One day, being exasperated she took some lethal step to lose her life. She hanged herself to death. But a polygamous society never hesitates in marrying twice. Immediately after her death, Kannamma kept persuading her son to remarry. She was not least affected by her daughter-in-law's death and on the top of it, she resisted her son from continuing to express grief for his dead wife.

Sivakami here tries to covey her message to society, a man is free to keep as many women as he wants for his physical service and colourful pleasures but these women are bereft from such freedom because of the discriminatory nature of society. It manifests on this brutal system bringing us close to see how the system provides full freedom to men in everything. The novelist has decried the Dalit movement and brings forth the true face of a Dalit patriarchy through a feminist lens. By depicting so many characters, she has explored the hidden face of unjust justice prevailed in the caste-ridden society.

CHAPTER 7

Critiquing Bama's *Sangati* and *Karukku*

Bama's *Sangati*

The dalit female writers' works render a different set of world comparatively to their male counterparts. Their works express their own as well the entire community's plight. Whatever Bama here narrates in her work *Sangati* is the fusion of facts and fiction. She herself has encountered excess humiliations, tortures, and oppression in a caste hierarchal society. She delineates how even Christianity ruined them. The advent of western civilisation disappointed Indian Dalit women. When British administrators came to India through trade about in the fourteenth century, they started making Indians slave and its effects suppressed more women especially Christian converted women remained at its bottom.

The Christian missionaries allured Dalit women to convert to Christianity on the pretext of free education, wealth, and removal of caste stigma. But converted women became more vulnerable. Later, it evoked in them a sense of protest against these atrocities. The novelist Bama was one such victim of the colonial change whose account has been penned down in her semi-autobiographical genre, *Sangati* (2005). Bama in *Sangati* has examined the cruel and unjust face of a society which suppresses marginalised women through multiple patriarchal structures. Bama Faustina Soosairaj is a dalit Tamil feminist novelist who was born in 1958, in a Paraiya family and is a converted dalit Christian writer. Her family converted from Hinduism to Christianity when the Christian mission beguiled them in the name of free education and other facilities to overcome their existing poverty. According to Bama, no other community converted to Christianity except her own paraiya community. She gained recognition for three widely known novels; *Karukku* (1992), *Sangati* (1994), and *Venmam* (2002). She also worked as a nun for a few months. Although she won Crossword Award for her autobiographical masterpiece of literature *Karukku* in 2000, it created immense controversy due to her explicit depiction of upper class atrocities on the dalits. Her first testimonial novel *Karukku* depicts the true picture of Bama's own life, her conversion (paraiya caste) to the Christian religion as well as caste patriarchy.

Bama's work *Sangati* captures the collective stories of several families and their day-to-day life minutely and can be called an autobiography of the entire community. *Sangati* first appeared in Tamil in 1994, and later it appeared in English in 2005. The novel is a critique of caste discrimination, Christian patriarchy as well as Dalit and Brahminical patriarchy. The title of *Sangati* refers to news, events, and happenings. Bama, in this novel, has examined the Dalit life from a feminist perspective along with the portrayal of patriarchy, caste, and communities during the British era. Vellaiyamma Kizhavi, Bama's grandmother narrates past events of dalit women. The novel unfolds how rituals and ceremonies are performed only by women among dalit families in a distinct way. The theme of this novel is the suppression and decline of dalit women in a caste-ridden society of Tamil Nadu. The tone is in a confessional mode since it documents the true image of a caste-ridden society.

She explains how she could not overcome caste, gender, and class hierarchy which were old norms of society. She felt that Dalits were cheated by religious conversions. Being a dalit, Bama closely has witnessed numerous incidents related to the lives of dalit women which she has articulated in the following words:

> My mind is crowded with many anecdotes: stories not only about the sorrows and tears of Dalit women, but also their lively and rebellious culture; their eagerness not to let life crush or shatter them, but rather to swim vigorously against the tide; about the self-confidence and self-respect that enables them to leap over their adversities by laughing at and ridiculing them; about their passion to live life with vitality, truth, and enjoyment; about their hard labour. I wanted to shout out these stories. (Bama 2005: xvi)

She aimed to throw light on the miserable condition of dalit women and inspire them to fight against injustices, both at home and in society. *Sangati* chronicles the false patriarchal system of a church where dalit women were being befooled in the name of god. Bama encountered the biased rules and regulations of a church where the rules favoured the upper caste people. Bama once joined the job as a nun to become a saviour for dalit children but the biased system of dominant Christians compelled her to resign that job. She could not find a place where she could relieve herself from the established discriminatory social structures. White patriarchy had crushed her dream. In the nineteenth century, Bama's family converted to Christianity in the hope that they will no longer face caste and gender discrimination. However, their aspirations did not yield positive results and they even lost some of the privileges of the dalit caste system. Converted Dalit Christians were being cheated even in the church which was a sacred place. She realised that it was only upper caste Christians who gained from Dalit conversion. These poor people were made to believe that God came only through the upper Christian people and were tricked into serving the priests.

In *Sangati* Bama has illustrated the hypocritical norms of Christian patriarchy where dalit women are exploited. Dalit women were asked to sweep the church. Once Bama rebelled against such unjust norms but was defeated in her purpose. She introspected the position of upper castes nuns. She assessed the precariousness of being a dalit. Here, she talks of the pitiable condition of dalit woman:

> The position of women being both pitiful and humiliating, really. In the fields they have to escape from upper caste men's molestations. At church, they must lick the priest's shoes and be his slaves while he threatens them with tales of God, Heaven, and Hell. Even when they go to their own homes, before they had a chance to cook some kanji or lie down and rest a little, they have to submit themselves to their husbands' torments. (Bama 2005: 35)

Bama is concerned for dalit woman's thrashed body. She has to bear children from time to time, which is a big barrier to her good health. They are not availed healthier nutrients to compensate the wrecked body. A huge number of dalit women die at childbirth or post delivery. So far as birth control is concerned, their men don't care about it. They just want pleasure. By the way, family lineage is dependent upon women but they are bereft of infrastructures. Being a dalit Christian, Bama narrates the suffocating life of all dalit Christian women. She articulates that such women undergo traumatic situation everywhere; at home by their own male counterparts, in the field through landowners, and at Church through a priest and other upper caste people who govern Church. She yearns for the lost dalit autonomous life which provides women a free place while Christian rules further marginalised them. In the name of religion, dalit women were being exploited with the imposition of certain codes of living.

In this way, dalit Christian women remained highly vulnerable on the basis of caste and gender.

Gender discrimination is also a crucial factor among dalits which has been reflected in *Sangati.* Bama comes up with her own observation regarding gender discrimination in dalit families that emerges with the earliest stage of life, and where special attention is provided for baby boys. If a baby girl cries, she is not fed immediately but if it is a boy, he is picked up instantly and given milk. Boys are considered of greater value in dalit families as well. Boys are given special nursing and proper health care. When the babies grow, different norms are set for females. So, a girl is expected to stay at home and perform all the household chores. So, a dalit girl never gets the pleasures of childhood freedom. Here, Bama narrates her own exploitation during her childhood days as to how her Patti (grandmother) was partial with her grandsons:

> She cared for her grandsons much more than she cared for us. If she brought anything home when she returned from work, it was always the grandsons she called first. If she brought cucumbers, she scooped out all the seeds with her finger nails, since she had no teeth, and gave them the remaining fruit. If she brought mangoes, we only got the skin, the stones, and such; she gave the best pieces of fruit to the boys. Because we had no other way out, we picked up and ate the leftover skins. (07- 08)

Michael S. Kimmel in *The Gendered Society* has rightly observed family as an institution that renders unequal gender relations, "Families are gendered institutions; they reproduce gender differences and gender inequalities among adults and children alike. Families raise children as gendered actors and remind parents to perform appropriate gender behaviours [...] each specific aspect of family life---marriage, child-rearing, housework, divorce---express the differences and inequalities of gender" (Kimmel 2008: 138). While narrating the oppression of Mariamma, Bama brings to light such gender violence as well as caste violence, a heinous crime of both the family as well as the society that punishes innocent dalit girls. Mariamma is a poor girl who goes to the field to gather firewood. An upper caste owner Kumarasami tries to sexually assault Mariamma when she goes to quench her thirst from his pump set after gathering her wood. When she escapes from his jaw he starts spreading rumours to blame her. So, the next day when Mariamma goes to the field to gather wood, Manikkam, a dalit boy merely talks to her simply joking with her but Kumarasami complains to the head of Dalit community and accuses them of obscenity.

When the meeting is called, Mariamma remains silent due to the fear of backlash. Her father slaps her publicly and threatens to kill her. Although the Dalit women attempt to prove Mariamma's innocence, all efforts go in vain and they are silenced by their own people saying, "Will you she-donkeys get out of here or do we have to stamp on you? The more we drive the wretches away, the more they come back and make trouble" (23). Younger women kept persuading Patti, the eldest woman, to go near to the panchayat and disclose the reality but she denied from speaking before them saying, "You talk as if it's all a game. Big woman, small woman, nonsense! Once you are born a woman, can you go and confront a group of four and five men? Should you even do it?" (28). The narrator could not let go unnoticed Patti's statements and she interrupted her, "From the time we are babies you treat boys in one way and girls in quite another. It's you folk who put butter in one eye and quicklime in the other" (29). She further extends the discrimination assigned on girls, to her Patti, satirically:

> Why can't we be the same as boys? We are not allowed to talk loudly or laugh noisily; even when we sleep we can't stretch out on our backs nor lie face down on our bellies. We always have to walk with our heads bowed down, gazing at our toes. You tell us all this rubbish and keep us under control. Even when our stomachs are screaming with hunger, we mustn't eat first. We are allowed to eat only after the men in the family have finished and gone. What, Patti, aren't we also human beings? (29)

The entire Dalit community is aware of Mariamma and Manikkam's innocence, yet they remain silent due to the fear of upper caste violence. A dalit girl's more suppression is unveiled when even Mariamma's own father asks her to apologise to the panchayat, "Well girl, you heard what he said, didn't you? Why are you standing there like a stone then? Beg forgiveness, you bitch, I have suffered enough shame because of you" (23). Once the judgement is passed, Manikkam is asked to pay only Rs.100, while Mariamma Rs. 200. Therefore, Bama draws our attention to the fact that an innocent dalit girl can be victimised without any fault and society remains a mute spectator. Here Spivak's theory 'can the subaltern speak?' is relevant wherein she says that subaltern women cannot retaliate against the oppression inflicted upon them. They can speak but they can't, because our society doesn't want them to speak. Spivak has rightly observed that subaltern women are more vulnerable to patriarchal atrocities. "There is no space from which the sexed subaltern subject can speak" (Spivak 1998: 307). At last, after this humiliation, Mariamma is married to Manikkam because no boy would marry a disgraced girl like her.

Bama, in *Sangati,* has attempted in a very elaborative way to document the prevalent notion of defilement and pollution of dalit women through sexuality. There are several characters in *Sangati* who are victimised on the basis of sexuality. Mariamma, an innocent poor girl is such a victim when she is alleged deliberately of sexual crime to a dalit boy Manikkam. Mariamma eventually had to sacrifice her entire life with Manikkam marrying him simply because society had taken her a polluted girl and nobody would marry such a girl. Although it was against Mariamma's happiness, she attempted a lot not to marry that boy but her Patti and father decided her future, finding no other alternative in a patriarchal based society. Her life was not in her hand, she had to bow down before social decisions. Such an incident reflects that every stage of a girl's growth the code origins from the social mechanism. Her every desire is choked through social laws. Our society expects a woman to have control over her sexuality, to obey all the established patriarchal structures without any hesitation. The other character, Esakki, also had to undergo the social punishment of patriarchal society when she eloped from her house and married a boy outside her caste. Her brothers eventually kill her even while she is carrying a baby inside her stomach because according to them having inter-caste sexual intercourse brings pollution in their family as well in the community. In this way, the observation over sexuality proves that women's sexual freedom is denied in all communities whether it is higher caste people or dalits.

Bama also draws attention to Dalit girls' gender oppression by describing the traumatic life of Esakku. She raises the issue of inequality within the Dalit community with specific reference to the question of marriage. She is of the view that Dalit girls don't enjoy the same rights given to the dalit boys. Society hardly taunts a dalit boy on doing inter-caste marriage but the same society hurls abuses if dalit girls do the same thing. Bama decries this biased attitude of inter-caste marriages that favour men. As she says, "When it comes to inter-caste marriages, our people are not bothered if boys make a marriage outside their caste. But if a girl marries out of caste no one will accept it. They'll make a big quarrel out of it" (106). She narrates the tragic condition of Esakku who elopes with her lover due to the opposition from her brother. Her brother tricks her and brutally kills her upon her return. After the gruesome murder, the restless spirit of

Esakku turns into a ghost and begins to chase every woman to give her cradle for her infant. Such is the fate of a dalit girl who marries secretly. Bama presents the harsh reality of a dalit woman's life where she is not allowed to take any decisions and is subjected to serious punishment for revolting against hypocritical traditions. Meena Kandasamy, a feminist novelist, poet, and critic, also condemns this biased system of marriage and gives her view that women are sexually oppressed when they are denied the choice of marrying a man outside her community and caste. Sharmila Rege, the other feminist critic also puts her argument by saying that there is a need to 'reclaim Ambedkar' and use his theoretical analysis to understand how certain norms as patriarchy, and particularly 'Brahminical patriarchy' operate to oppress Dalit women.

Bama has intricately explored gender discrimination of dalit women and presented their trials in *Sangati.* She interprets that women who work as building site labourers, factory workers, and field workers are given lesser wages than men. She is deeply tormented by the disparities between men and women in financial matters and contends that men are free to spend money whatsoever they earn according to their own while women are forced to carry the burden of a family. She instructs all dalit women:

> We have to labour in the fields as hard as men do, and then on top of that, struggle to bear and raise our children. As for the men, their work ends when they've finished in the fields. If you are born into this world, it is best you were born a man. Born as women, what do we get? We only toil in the fields and in the home until our vaginas shrivel". (6)

So, it can be said that despite the implementation of the Equal Remuneration Act in 1976, women are still marginalised in private sectors and marginalised women face deeper injustices due to which they continue to remain at the lowest rungs of society.

Bama was concerned about why peys possession is only to women especially dalit women. Most of the time, her eyes perceived dalit women's peys possession and their suffering during such a period. One day, she could not help inquiring into this issue to her Patti. Her Patti convinced her in a traditional mind, a mind that believed in orthodoxical norms:

> It is our women who go off on their own to work in the jungles and in the fields. Those are the places where peys like to wander about. The peys catch the women when they are alone, without a circle of friends or relations. If they are menstruating, or if they are terrified in the first place, definitely the peys will catch hold of them. Of course, peys would catch

> upper caste women too if they were to go out to work as we do. It's just that they don't catch men. And that's because men don't carry the same fear in their hearts. End they won't catch women either, if they dare to walk past without fear. (58)

Bama's heart could not get convinced on her Patti's illogical and superstitious thoughts. She herself started wondering over it. It appalled her why every spirit is afraid of men and not women; why woman is categorised as the weakest creature? Examining such old proverbs and norms she arrived at the conclusion of women's psychology. It is a societal notion that Dalit woman is regarded more polluted and vulnerable in menstruation cycle and they are easily possessed by peys. Bama has also examined such possession of peys during women's menstruation cycle why only lower caste women get possessed and not upper caste women. She heard people say peys possess only dalit women because they go outside to work and next when they are alone. The upper caste women don't have to undergo the same problem because they live within their homes and are always surrounded by people. If they had to go in fields for work they also would be victims of such possession. But after a close observation, Bama reaches to the conclusion that all such belief is false; the crux of this possession is dalit women's psychological as well as physical stresses who indulge in works both inside along with the outside continuously. She is grieved at the multiple burdens that the dalit women carry. Their husbands pester them when they are home and they have to bear back-breaking works at fields where they can't escape from the landlords' physical and psychological assaults. Even after their long day works, they don't get time to have a sigh of relief in the evening because of the household works would be waiting for them. She further writes, "Night after night they must give in to their husband's pleasure...the stronger ones somehow manage to survive all this. The one who don't have the mental strength are totally oppressed; they succumb to mental ill-health and act as if they are possessed by peys". (59)

Bama asserts that such distress is not with upper caste women because they are not laden with such mental as well as physical pressures. She comes up with her observation that even dalit men are not possessed by peys because they are not afraid of it. They also work hard in the fields but they still have freedom at home in the evening. She is surprised to know that a man bravely strikes at peys when they possess women to recover them. She warns very strongly the women of her community to be conscious of such stupid beliefs of peys possession during menstruation or in general days. She boosts up dalit women to change their orthodox mentality if they desire to be courageous women. She appeals to all dalit women in a moral tone to destroy all old illusions, to be strong in the following thought-provoking words:

> We must be strong. We must show by our own resolute lives that we believe ardently in our independence. I told myself that we must never allow our minds to be worn out, damaged and broken in the belief that this is our fate. Just as we work hard so long as there is strength in our bodies, so too, must we strengthen our hearts and minds in order to survive. (59)

Bama views Dalit woman's life gets worse if she does not resist her husband's misbehaviour. She brings forth the true painful mishappening of her mother's sister Perimma who was butchered by her husband who was a drunkard. When asked by Bama, her Patti said, "I reared a parrot and handed it over to be mauled by a cat. Your Periappan (the victim's husband) beat her to death. My womb, which gave birth to her, is still on fire. He killed her so outrageously, the bastard" (10). But why did he beat her to death, Bama once again extended the query? Without making a delay she replied, "You ask me why? Because the man was crazy with lust. Because he wanted her every single day. How could she agree to his frenzy after she worked all hours of the day and night, inside the house and out? He was an animal. When she refused, he practically broke her in half. Once in my presence, he hit her with the rice-pounder" (10). Bama's own grandmother had got Perimma married at a very early age. Perimma's husband was a man of an animalistic nature. In the words of Patti, her husband wanted to make with her every night but once she refused, he cracked her dead. Patti was too grieved on such a painful death of her daughter that she was almost cursing her son-in-law. While asking by Bama why no one took any action at such brutal life of her aunt? Patti remained stunt for a while but slowly broke her silence by uttering how other people could have protected her from the jaw of such an animalistic person who could not spare others and rather started bellowing at them saying, "She is my wife, I can beat her or even kill her if I want" (11). So, how could one have protected her, says Patti?

Bama was tormented internally when once she as a little school-going girl, saw the animalistic beatings and whippings of another character, Thaayi, by her husband. Her heart became heavy and horrified at such a painful sight of wife-battering and whipping. Bama's observation draws our attention here to the life of a woman in her role as a wife. She throws light on Thaayi's personality. Thaayi was a beautiful and simultaneously innocent woman blessed with the lightest-skinned colour of her entire area. When she dressed herself up, she looked completely a distinct woman from all women of her area. Owing to her attractive personality, she received extra attention from people. The patriarchal forces dragged her to marry a person whom she didn't like at all. Although she was not a woman of bad character or immoral behaviour what her husband thought of her. Bama is much grieved while narrating such a dead life of Thaayi. Thaayi's husband usually beat her heavily with a belt. His violent nature left uncountable scarce on her body due to his severe strapping. When Bama came close to her, her eyes filled with tears; she could not take her tears back into her eyes. This haunting sight of wife battering overcame her so much so that it remained in her subconscious over a long time. A neighbour Karuthumuthu tried to protect Thaayi, forbidding her husband, "Are you a human being or what, da? Isn't there a limit to how much you hit a woman? You are killing her like this, without any pity" (43). She saw Thaayi's husband retorting Karuthumuthu who protested against such hitting in enraged words, "Who are you to speak for this munde? She's my wife, I can beat her or kill her if I wish. You go and mind your own business" (43). Rather to understand the situation or consider his words, he more violently began to hurl out abusive words at Thaayi, "You common whore, you, any passing loafer will come in support for you, you mother fucker's daughter. You will go with ten men!" (43)

When Bama narrated this torturous incident to her mother, her mother began to make her understand with a heavy sigh, "It's as if you become a slave from the very day you are married. That's why all men scold their wives and keep them well under control". (43). Bama was questioning to her mother how a man can surpass all humanity with his wife simply because he has tied a *tali* around her neck. Tying *tali* does not mean that a man is free to punish his wife as much as he wishes, asks Bama? The pitiable life of Thaayi moved Bama extremely and compelled her to go again to see her pathetic interwoven life. Thaayi's husband crosses the conventionality of humanity when he cuts all the head-hair of his wife and hangs down in front of his door. The next day, when Bama was crossing against

Thaayi's door, she noticed a big chunk of hair hanging down at her threshold. Then she saw Thaayi spreading her paddy to dry. The odd scene of a big hunk of hair makes her ask about it to Thaayi. So, she called her to know about that hair hanging down. But before she could explain anything regarding it, her husband came out from the house and retorted by intervening them, "The thing is *Madani*, I wanted four or five people like you to ask exactly that and to spit in her face. It's this whore's hair that I've cut off myself and hung there. Look at her neck--- you won't find a single hair left. I cut her hair off to put down her pride" (43). Bama, after having observed with her naked eyes such violent attitude of man towards a woman makes her poignant. Theses poignant crisis of women was haunting in her sharp mind that ask several questions to her soul. She couldn't help without asking multi-questions to her mother why a woman like Thaayi tolerates all the tortures through their man? Why doesn't such a woman leave her husband if he beats her all the time? If she escapes from the trapping of a brutal husband at least she would not have to encounter all types of man-violence?

As soon as Bama puts these questions before her mother, her mother convinces her, marriage is not a rope of sands which can be broken easily. She explains to Bama, "It's not easy to get away, once you are married. Once you've put your head in the mortar, can you escape from the pestle? No, she must continue to suffer until her head rests on the earth at last" (44). After having been explained by her mother, Bama's heart was crowded with a series of emotions. All types of resentment, resistance, excitement, anger, and hatred grew to govern her mind. For some time it made her hover. She was against embracing such menial attitudes of society because every society is a product of man-made not female. Talking about the plight of Dalit women, Bama makes her thought-provoking statement:

> All women are slaves to men, our women really are the worst sufferers. It is not the same for women of other castes and communities. Our women cannot bear the torment of upper caste masters in the fields, and at home, they cannot bear the violence of their husbands". (65)

To speak in non-Christian dalit context, the patriarchal structure is loose prevailing among them, it is in a sense not institutionalised norms of obeying her husband. They are not in a way forced upon to consider their husband as deities. A dalit woman among Chakkiliya or Pallar communities finishes her relation with her husband when she finds life hard to lead with him. Pechhiamma in *Sangati* is a strong example of it. She marries second time by finishing her relationship with her husband after he beats her brutally on a regular dose. It is upper caste people who allege stigma an abandoned woman or consider a widow impure. As she says to her mother:

> Quite true, Akka. In the upper castes, too, a woman can't lead a life on her own if she has left her husband. on all sides, they'll call her an abandoned wife and her life will be finished. It doesn't matter whether she comes from a wealthy family, whether she is beautiful, whether she is educated or ignorant; the day she leaves her husband, she loses everything". (95)

Bama remorsefully realises, it is only with dalit converted Christian women who can't marry twice if her first husband is alive. Bama while communicating to her mother throws light on Christian patriarchal domination in the marriage system. She favours non-Christian norms that at least give full freedom to women. She heard non-Christian women, "They say that when a man dislikes his wife if her hand touches it's a sin if her foot touches him it's a sin. So, if a husband nags and finds fault all the time with whatever you do or try, it makes no difference whether you live with him or leave him. But in our Christian religion, you can't leave a husband go off on your own that easily" (94). Such Bible follower women cannot even think of leaving her husband. Once the *tali* is tied around their neck, it is the end of her life. "The priest blesses with the tali by saying neither law nor panchayat nor courts of justice can separate a wedded couple" (94). She is expected to spend her entire life with her husband whether life is a bed of roses or thorns. She has to tolerate all types of tortures to the last breath of life.

Bama concerns the pervasive lethal practices in the system of marriage. While communicating with her mother she discovers the traditional mindset of societal people. She utters why only a woman's prestige dwells in her marriage and virginity? She is extremely upset while disclosing patriarchal power. Marriage is also a social and familial bond among non-Christian dalit families but not as such as it occurs between dalit Christians. Although dalit women neither follow strictly all the established marriage rules nor are they subservient to their husbands nevertheless there are certain behaviours of men through which such women are impinged upon. Bama has explored dalit women's oppression mostly from Christian point of view where a woman is tied with all restrictions. She reveals the rules of living of non-Christian dalits are slightly different. Although marriage without a guardian's consent is also problematic among non-Christian dalits the issue does not get complicated like that of dalit Christians. If a non-Christian dalit girl flees with a boy, a panchayat is called and the dispute is settled down with some affordable fines by allowing them to marry. So, dalit women's life is independent in many ways. The case is not the same with dalit Christian women. They have to go according to their parents and priest's rules. That is why Bama repents for why her family converted to Christian. At the end of the novel, she has reflected critical views of her family converted to Christianity by losing all the independent facilities of dalits. She realises that non-Christian dalits are lucky who are not bound with certain laws of independent life in every step. Even Bama's mother regrets for her mistake of adopting Christian community. The novelist's regret is reflected in her words full of grief, "Had we stayed as Hindus, our women would have had the chance of divorce at least" (97). She now feels that the missionaries had separated them in the name of party, priest, God, and caste; they have become like grinning puppets in their hands. They had befooled them by taking away their primary rights from them as well as marginalised them even in the outside world. She appeals to all dalit women of new generations that they must start thinking in their new ways by taking decisions, "Don't we sharpen and renew a rusted sickle? Just like that, we must sharpen our minds and learn to live with self-respect". (104)

Bama's female characters are victimised by the stigmatic notion of caste. Caste impinges a certain mode of living for dalit women. Unless the prejudice of caste is rooted out dalit women will always remain under the constant fear of sexual abuse. In the words of Kancha Ilaiah, the most requisite solution to remove caste prejudices is that all castes, upper and lower should be dalitised. When all will labour equally, the inequality stuck with dalits may come to an end (cited in Chakravarti 2013: 87). *Sangati* reflects how dalit women and their activities are perceived by the patriarchal world. According to Bama, the conjugal fight is no exception among dalits, it occurs even among upper caste family but they do all things within their four walls silently, do not let others know. She says that upper caste women totally submit to their husbands as 'a cobra shrinks into its box'. But it is a fact that a dalit woman doesn't tolerate her husband's single unfit word. Bama defends dalit women on the basis of wage-earning. She comes up with her own observation that in some of dalit family women run house; men do not provide money to maintain their living. That is why, in such circumstances, a man doesn't deserve to dominate his woman; so why she will swallow all the hot words of her man. Bama clearly has castigated on upper caste women's ways of living how they behave with their husbands, how they follow all the obligations of their husbands, how they maintain all the Brahminical codes imposed upon them. She has tried to reflect dalit women's lack of facilities such as their separate bathroom and washroom. Upper caste women easily find available separate rooms for everything; they keep a separate room for cooking, bathing, sleeping, and worshipping. She digs out her observation that dalit women are deprived of such comforts; their critical situation compels them to go outside for every work like washing clothes, relieving themselves, bathing, and any other work.

Bama has presented dalit women as victims mostly through external patriarchies; since at home they easily handle conflict with their men behaving tit-for-tat. Their main oppression takes place outside their home where they become puppets in the hands of dominant men. She discloses that it is Brahminical patriarchy that imposes upon upper caste women to stick to particular codes of husband-worship. But dalit women are generally stress-free from such husband-worship. While talking about the plight of dalit women due to dowry, Bama openly tells us dalits hardly fight for dowries. They do not mind whatever the bride party gives to the groom's party during the marriage.

Gabriele Dietrich is absolutely right when she comes up with her observation pertaining to dalit women's tortures through dowry, in her essay "Dalit Movements and Women's Movement". In this essay, she has traced that it is true that violence against upper caste women like cases of dowry bound with torture, separation of spouses, suicide, and murder frequently occur more among them. Family violence occurs frequently within the upper caste family. Such type of family violence occurs to some extent less within dalit family; tortures for dowry do not turn menace in dalits. Sharmila Rege contradicts the ideas of Dietrich when she in her essay "Dalit Women Talk Differently (1998)" gives her personal opinion on dalit women's oppression. Rege, in this essay, tells us that dalit women have to confront more violence than upper caste women in the connection of dowry, deaths, and violent controls and regulations on the mobility and sexuality by the family as well as collective rape (43). Her observation regarding the collective rape of dalit women is correct but her observation that the dowry issue is more problematic among dalit than the upper caste families does not seem correct because we know dalit people easily get married on a little dowry. We see in our society, the more a family is highly prosperous the more it demands dowry, the more they torture their women for dowry and keep them under restrictions. Bama contends that dalit women confront less domestic violence compared to the upper caste women for the sake of dowry demands. She asks us to have a look at the birth of a girl in the upper caste family how they mourn the arrival of a girl. She goes on to say that they are grieved at the birth of a girl because they are trapped while providing a big amount of dowry. She comes at conjectural ideas that the issue of dowry doesn't become the cause of death for dalit women. Among dalits, the bride party provides whatever little things they can afford, and rest of the things are maintained by the groom's party. But the value of all women even through marriage is measured on the basis of patriarchal control in all castes.

Bama appeals to all dalit people not to copy the ways of living of upper caste people since living as dalit they have their own pleasure. She is prompting dalit women through her aid *Sangati*. As a female dalit writer she herself has encountered all the miseries and ups and down as a dalit woman. Her teaching is much pertinent to all dalit women, "Men can humiliate us a thousand times, speak about us with disrespect, and act towards us in that way too. And that is accepted as normal. But let a woman be outspoken just once--- just once a single time--- let her act just once with self-respect. He will never stand for it" (122). She wants dalit women to overcome firmly this unjust patriarchal world with great fortitude. She desires to bring a new discourse in women's existing thoughts; women should change their mentality in a new way. She boosts up dalit women through the following courageous words:

> If we ourselves do not change our condition, then who will come and change it for us? We must give up the belief that a married life of complete service to a man is our only fate. We must change this attitude that if married life turns to be a perpetual hell, we must still grit our teeth and endure it for a lifetime. We must bring up our girls to think in these new days from an early age. We should educate boys and girls alike, showing no difference between them as they grow into adults. We should give our girls the freedom we give our boys. (123)

She expects a gender-free society. She requests dalit people to bring a new mind-set to society by bringing up boys and girls with no difference because gender discrimination beginning from infancy leads to a form of venom for women. Boys and girls should be given equal freedom to get an opportunity in education. If boys and girls are reared equally women will definitely get an opportunity to present their strength vigorously. In this way, all the hierarchal violence, injustice, and inequalities will come to an end. Here Bama's words show her motive behind this novel, "And the saying will come true that 'women can make and women can break'. I am hopeful that such a time will come soon" (123). All in all, it can be said without any least doubt that Bama's lesson in *Sangati* is to educate, agitate and organise.

Bama's *Karukku*

Bama's next novel, *Karukku,* focuses on her own plight as well the plight of her entire community largely through Christianity. It is completely her autobiographical text. This book won her Crossword Awards in 2001. This book was originally written in Tamil language and subsequently it was translated into other languages. While writing this book, Bama broke the stereotypical beliefs of her family as we as the nation. She unhesitantly has delineated the casteist world where marginalised groups of people are humiliated on the basis of caste. Very rigidly, she has unmasked the barriers faced in her life imposed by the caste system which compels her to question why there is one system for one lower man and the other for the upper caste? There is nothing like exaggeration in portraying the tortures, violence, and humiliation of dalit people in this documentary.

She has just chronicled all the incidents in her life in a caste-discriminatory society. It throws light on caste, a persisting reality in our society and inter-caste fights among other people. She inevitably sketches out, a soul born as untouchable has to survive on the fringe of society, it no longer becomes the part of mainstream society. The narrator itself is the writer who manifests all the important milestones in her life since her childhood to adult. In another way, we can say, this novel is the growth of the novelist's mind. Born in an untouchable family she confronted the embedded discriminatory system of Church organisation, at educational places, as well as other private and government sectors. She says, she didn't know about untouchability until she joined a school. During class three once she was crossing through the road after leaving the school hanging a bag on her shoulder. It usually took her approximately twenty minutes to reach home. Her eyes were observing all the activities and fun acted by the people when she crossed through the road; how upper caste people mocked her and separated themselves from her mere touch.

Most of the lands belonged to the Naicker community. And all the marginalised people had to be their employees in their fields. Bama's own mother and grandmother were working for the Naickers for their survival. She was grieved when she saw even a Naicker's newly born child calling her mother and grandmother by their name as if they are lords and these poor women are their slaves. While her grandmother, like any other labourer would address that little boy Ayya, Master, and followed his order. It was an extremely shameful phenomenon to see for the novelist. As a little girl she also sometimes accompanied her grandmother and mother to the field where they worked. Whenever her grandmother (Patti) and mother felt thirst, the Naicker's wife poured water from a distance with a cup and they sipped it through their own palm not touching the cup as it would pollute the cup. The narrator felt extremely disgusted when her eyes fell on such horrific discrimination.

As soon as the dawn broke, her Paatti got up instantly and took the way for Naicker's home that was her regular work. She cleaned the dispersed cow-dung, and cleaned the door there. Then she was given the stale pieces of roti and some rice, curry which she brought for the family. Sometimes the narrator realised that the brought food by her Paatti was nothing but the worst and smelled food which Naicker's wife were supposed to throw into the dustbin. Once, the narrator herself accompanied her Patti to the Naicker's house to receive the food. She observed her Patti placing her plate and then Naicker's wife transferred the leftover foods to Patti's plate from a distance, it seemed even the plate touching would bring them a sense of defilement. It was bizarre for her confronting such tragedy. When the narrator instructed her Patti to stop begging before the Naicker, her Patti retorted to her in a very simple term, "These people are the maharajas who feed us our rice. Without them, how will we survive? Haven't they been upper caste from generation to generation, and haven't we been lower caste? Can we change this?" (Bama 2012: 17)

The next incident she narrates of her brother's encountered discrimination. As a university student, her brother Annan was coming home during holidays. While visiting the nearby village library, on his way, a Naicker following him came to him and asked his name. Her brother replied to him 'Anna'. Merely name could not contend that Naicker and so extendingthe talk he tried to know of his street. That man more probably groped him to know the caste. But as soon as Annan retorted them, "I am a Paraya from the Cheri Street" it jolted that man and he stalked off immediately. The matter didn't get buried at that point but that Naicker dragged it before Annan's Paatti when she, next day, turned up the Naicker's field. He complained about Annan's harsh reply. Paatti also justified her grandson's harsh reply to that Naicker, saying his grandson is an educated college boy and thus how could he tolerate any unfit words of others?

The next incident of Annan makes us aware when he was searching out his books in the library, he deliberately added the title, M.A. with his name. The attendant's eyes went on M.A. and immediately he brought him a tool to sit on, and further began addressing him as 'sir'. When Annan narrated of such respect to his sister, her happiness knew no bounds. And he also instructed the narrator in a very encouraging tone:

> Because we are born into the Paraya Jati, we are never given any honour or dignity, or respect. We are stripped of all that, But if we study and make progress, we can throw away these indignities. So study with care, learn all you can. If you are always ahead in your lessons, people will come to you of their own accord and attach themselves to you. Work hard and learn. (18)

These impressive words proved to be a magic in a very impressive way on the narrator's mind and it encouraged her to learn more and more from all sides. She started studying carefully and passed her exam with first division. Now many classmates intimating her made her friend even though she was a Paraiya. She was annoyed looking at the biased attitudes of teachers with untouchable students. If anything bad was done in the school, they unhesitantly blamed untouchable students. Bama here narrates one of such a disgusting incident when she was a young student. As usual, she was playing with her classmates in the playground. The game was, one had to run right up the coconut palm and touch its tip. In between playing such a game, a coconut fell from the tree above her head. She was startled to see it. She first looked at that coconut, it was half ripped and half raw and she left it there. Everyone started raising their finger against her saying it was she who plucked that coconut. Fearing of it she left the coconut there and ran home straight. The next morning when she turned to her school, the headmaster abruptly calling her insulted her uttering, "You have shown us your true nature as a Paraya. You climbed the coconut tree yesterday after everybody else had gone home, and you stole a coconut. We can't allow you inside this school. Stand outside" (19). She was embarrassed because the headmaster was shrieking at her in front of all the children. Now she became the subject of mockery and humiliation for other students. They just were staring at her and walking off to the class.

She dumbstruck stood there before the headmaster, not knowing what to do in such a situation. She was being targeted without her fault. After a while the other teacher came near to her and asked her if she wanted to save herself she must go through a confession. So, she will have to go to the priest and confess her crime. The teacher very adamantly said to her to get a letter from the priest after confession and then she will again get entry into the school otherwise not. She was once again made scapegoat through the priest. When she narrated the truth to the priest that she had not stolen any coconut still she was being punished deliberatly. The priest didn't trust her yet. She begged before him to let her permission to get entry into the school but the priest on the contrary rebuked her, "After all, you are from the Cheri. You might have done it. You must have done it" (19). It appalled her and her eyes were discharging hot tears after listening to the priest's hot words. After much implore, the priest wrote her a letter to let her rejoin the school. Heaving sighs of relax, she turned to the school and handed it to the headmaster. The headmaster took the letter reluctantly and addressed her in some abusive language. Everyone in the classroom eyed her suddenly and it made her disgusted. She was feeling ashamed of her caste. Caste was the only barrier in her cheerful life. The teachers as well as the priest were torturing her on the pretext of caste. But confronting such obstructions she had grapplled all the difficulties. So, forgetting such a tragedy, she again began to concentrate on her further study. When she arrived in the high school, she was enrolled in a hostel. Humiliation and alienation also pursued her there in the hostel. The Warden-sister of the hostel didn't pay heed to the lower caste students what they paid lip service was only to the upper caste people. The narrator here unveils how the Warden-sister mistreated and misbehaved with the low caste students, "These people get nothing to eat at home; they come here and they grow fat" (20). When she returned to the school after holidays, the Warden-sister made derogatory remarks while frowning at them, "Look at the Cheri children! When they stay here, they eat their fill and look as round as potatoes. But look at the state in which they come from home – just skin and bone!" (20). It was really the toughest day for the narrator to confront such embarrassing comments.

Once, the narrator was travelling by a bus to home for holidays. A Naicker woman sitting next to her in the bus asked her where she had to drop? She replied to the woman, the Cheri. As soon as that woman heard the word 'Cheri' from the narrator's mouth, she left the seat and moved ahead to get the next seat. The upper caste people preferred to stand up all through the journey rather sit next to her. Being grieved, she here shares pains of being born in an untouchable family:

> In this society, if you are born into a low caste, you are forced to live a life of humiliation and degradation until your death. Even after death, caste-difference does not disappear. Whenever you look however much you study, whatever you take up, caste discrimination stalks us in every nook and corner and drives us into a frenzy. It is because of this that we are unable to find a way to study well and progress like everyone else. And this is why a wretched lifestyle is all that is left to us. If you are born into a low caste, every moment of your life is a moment of struggle. People screw up their faces and look at us with disgust the moment they know our caste. It is impossible to describe the anguish that look causes. But along with the anguish, there is anger too. What can our anger do to them, though? It seems we have to swallow our anger and just carry on with our troubled lives. (27)

Even if her family converted to Christianity, caste pursued them everywhere. The upper caste Christians had fenced their cemetery that was their own separate. The dalit corpses were not allowed to bury in the Christians' cemetery eventhough they all were Christians. The Christians also discriminated them everywhere. During the arrival of New Year, the priest tended to distribute New Year calendars. On asking for a calendar by the narrator, the priest immediately asked for money for the same calendar which he was distributing free. Thus, she remained deprived of getting that calendar. The narrator then went to the Reverend Mother who was distributing the holy picture and asked for the same. At this the Reverend Mother commented, "Have you given me some money in order to buy you holy pictures? Very well, now, you may all go home quickly without leaning on the walls or touching anything" (67). So, we can see how even the Church organisation was built upon hierarchal position, marginalising dalits.

After completing her B.ED, the narrator started looking for a job to sustain the miserable and poverty-stricken life. She then joined a convent as a nun and started teaching regularly. A wave of help for poor children was lying inside her body. There also she perceived how the poor people were being discriminated and thrashed by the teachers. The teachers didn't pay much heed to the poor children. The discriminatory nature of teachers measured one way to those who were the have and the other way to those who were have not. Eventually, the anarchy prevailing in that organisation compelled her to resign from that job. Sometimes she reached at the end of the tether realising that death would be better than living alive in such a discriminatory world where a man is measured on the basis of caste. Despite being a well-educated woman she was encountering humiliation and tortures like any other marginalised soul. She had thought previously perhaps getting a good education can change her life, it can change others' low views looking towards her but it was to no avail. She came across that caste as well as poverty were the major factors that were obstructing her life full of dignity. She utters the same anguish here, "Life is difficult if you happen to be poor, even though you are born into the upper castes. When this is the case, the condition of those who are born into the Paraya community, as the poorest of the poor, struggling for daily survival, doesn't need spelling out". (79)

Her conscience is battered to think how much poverty prevails inside the marginalised community? She takes a look at the upper caste living standards how their children are brought up in a luxurious way, achieve good education from the top institutes and universities. Their children wear fine and costly dress that separated them from poor students. The poor students' dirty and cheap dress marks their caste and class and simultaneously it draws the line of untouchability. She strongly asserts that the marginalised people have been tolerating such discrimination and suppression taking as their ultimate fate because they have on other way to grapple with it. Even if there are some educated people who are challenging against the prevailed social norms but how long they will be going on without food in their stomachs. Most of the marginalised people depend on upper castes for their earning, so where will they seek out the space to put out their anxiety and harassment. The wealthy have crushed out the poor thoroughly. The narrator is tormented by such unjust law and order in society. The conversion didn't benefit the author in any way. Here she tells us the encountered threads through church authority:

> Far worse is the attitude not only within our own church. They have made use of Dalits who are marginalised who are immersed in ignorance as their capital, set up a big business, and only profited their own castes. In the churches, dalits are the most in numbers alone. In everything else, they are the least. It is only the upper-caste Christians who enjoy the benefits and comforts of the church. Even amongst the priests and nuns, it is the upper castes who hold all the high positions, show off their authority, and throw their weight about. And if Dalits become priests or nuns, they are pushed aside and marginalised first of all, before the rest go about their business. It is because of this that even though dalits like me might wish to take up the path of renunciation, we find there is no place for us there. (80)

Dalits were even marginalised in the church on the pretext of narrating Scriptures and creating God's fear in their hearts. Such a phenomenon the narrator here delineates how Sisters forcibly made them convinced, "if they commit sins they have to write down all those sins and confess before God". All the nuns told them stories associated with the Devils and sins. Due to the aroused fear in her, the narrator followed blindly what the Sisters and their biased system asked her to do. The Sisters told these dalit people that if they sin, it must delight Devil's heart. They had put in a strong fear in the narrator's conscience and that's why whenever she by mistake stole a stick or pencil, if she didn't listen to her parents at home, if she made any mistake during school hour, a frightening image of the devil appeared before her eyes, laughing happily showing its teeth at her. Until she confessed even her false imagination, she was troubled and restless to come over it. She was made to believe that she as a dalit Christian can't touch the host at Communion. The Sisters had informed strictly that Jesus dwells inside that host, so no one can bite Him, nor should anyone can touch that host with their sinful hands otherwise blood would flow down from their hands. It was really a funny piety for the narrator but after all she had to go through all.

One day, the narrator made her mind touch the host with her finger fearlessly. So, she hid herself behind her head-cloth and touched quickly the host. The blood didn't flow from her hand. So, she thought it was of course false teachings of the Sisters for dalits only to marginalise them. The narrator when grew older, the Sisters stopped beating her with a stick but only shouted at her on little mistakes in a foul language. Since she was good at reciting the litany and so the Sisters asked her to recite the appropriate prayers before the girls who were supposed to get married. According to the norm, a catechist offered the lessons to the supposed grooms there in the church. The Sisters in the meanwhile checked their recitation and if they could not recite the prayer properly it was only the narrator who became the subject of punishment. Once, while reciting the prayers, Sister turned up suddenly and stood beside her that caused her nervousness and which led her commit a mistake. On changing the line by mistake, the Sister instantly gave her a big blow on her forehead. It left the narrator stunned, the pain arose as if she would die with it. This shows the cruel and unsympathetic treatment given to dalits at church.

When the narrator finished eighth class, she later joined the convent boarding school for the ninth class. Now she started discarding some fear of such Sisters and their stories of Devils from her mind. Subsequently, during the college term, she almost realised all the hypocritical attitudes of Sisters. If we find in the words of the narrator itself:

> It was during that time I was studying there that the love and devotion that I felt towards God gradually diminished. Of course, in times of trouble, I thought to myself, God helps me, but that was all. Everything became a matter of routine drudgery. All sorts of questions beset my mind, such as, 'Why should I go to Pusai every day? Why should I take Communion?' I began to think that the priests and nuns had deceived me hugely. Up to that time, I had thought that God came to me through these people, but this belief changed to the extent that I now began to feel strongly that God was not with them. And so I began to dislike everything they did. I began to question them. I argued and fought. I thought to myself with some disgust, Chi, they are all hypocrites and frauds. (102)

Now she is determined to communicate with God directly, not through Church or priest. Now, she no longer believed that God came only through church and priest. She perceived that God can be seen through one's mind, through one's good deeds. The false system of church was pushing her to the bottom of society. Everyone at church taught her, God is loving, gentle, kind, sympathetic, a forgiver who forgives all sinners. But nobody taught that God never likes injustice. God never likes discrimination. Nobody taught her that 'all is equal in God's eyes'. Nobody taught her God dwells even inside the untouchables' hearts. The untouchable oppressed people were kept ignorant from good teachings so that they would not object to their unjust rules, and biased orders. Now when the narrator has searched the truth, she looked at the church simply in terms of a place of religious conflicts. It is only the upper caste people who rule over the church, their kith, and kin. Those who hold power, rules, and orders are theirs. These powerful souls control over the poor by infusing some blind faiths in the name of God, while they themselves act differently. There was one system for the marginalised while the other for the rich. Now the Dalits have come to know the manipulation and deceitful acts of the upper caste authority.

Conclusion

The examinations and explorations on dalit women have discovered that it is impossible to get honour and respect for dalit women as long as they are laden with the economic crisis and dependent on the resources of upper caste people. A huge crowd of dalit women workers are unfortunately employed to such works which are devalued; like weeding, planting, harvesting, and some other building working activities. Kalpana and Vasanth Kannaabiran have rightly viewed, "Women at work can never quite escape being defined as sexual objects. Sexual access, ranging from small intimacies right through to actual intercourse is often assumed to be part of the working relationship" (2002: 85). Dalit women as workers are inevitably viewed as 'women of lose character' and thus they are more vulnerable. Their illegal sexual relationship is not always forceful but sometimes they willingly extend the relationship with other male counterparts. They fell forced to be separated from their husband and the family from morning to evening for fieldwork. While all the time conversing with male counterparts, repartee, flirtation, and fun rise between them and subsequently lead to physical relationship and sometimes with landowners. But the way they were sexually exploited in the past has changed. Earlier they made relationship without paying them but nowadays they do pay for the access they get from these women's body. Some dalit women sometimes become prey to prostitution and fall beneath a resort due to extreme poverty. They are sometimes dragged to consensual relations reluctantly simply because they belong to a different caste that is different from the dominant upper caste. Sometimes there is no way to overcome such a critical situation because there is nothing for survival for them.

The most degrading thing is that eventhough a dalit woman does the same work that a man does but she is paid less than a man because of gender basis. Such works degrade their respect. If dalit men want to protect their women from the cruelties of upper caste people, they should stop their women from working in the fields and other low category works like doing domestic jobs in others' houses where they are vulnerable. Such men themselves should change conservative thoughts of women's oppression. Men in an androcentric society let it go unnoticed when there is a domestic fight between women within the home. Hence, the burden of respect and dignity falls alone on women who dwell within the home.

Modesty and dignity are the certain terms applied to all women where dalit women's immodesty brings a big shame everywhere. Their outside field works compel them to mix freely with other male workers at their work place, so how could they separate from men's contact. Their lack of ignorance renders them lack of physical self-control and wrong dressing sense. Society labels them as immoral and wanton women. Their particular caste imparts an object of sexual property for whom they work, as they are not expected to follow the norms of stridharma. Socially subordinate position impinges them inherent moral deviant and polluted body. Likewise, dalit men too are emasculated by the upper caste men; they are forced to think that they are helpless in protecting their women's chastity or stridharma. So, dalit women should at first improve their living standards and proper way of wearing costumes. Their dress is sometimes dishevelled, hair untamed, sari without pin, language vulgar and they even do not bother of it and let it go unnoticed. A proper way of using language must be commanded by them. And all these codes of living can be rendered only through education that is in the Foucauldian concept 'knowledge is power'. Most of the Dalit people's real hardship lies in their ignorance. If they will be educated, their central difficulties will collapse. But the problem in our country is that even if some laborious and brilliant-minded people aspire for good education but their caste always creates hurdles in their ways. So, dalit people should be given caste free atmosphere to achieve education. Bama's own hard days of being a dalit girl student disclose all the hypocritical treatment of caste-based patriarchal society. She reminds us how when she as a dalit student was wandering hither and thither to heir a room while owners were not ready to avail her easily since she was an unmarried girl first and second she belonged to dalit caste. According to her, dalit women cannot set themselves free from all the biased structures of society until they themselves swear to bring changes.

If we examine a woman's identity in patriarchal society we come across, the identity of a woman invariably is known through her husband in most circumstances. In our country, most of the time a woman changes her surname when she gets married. On the other hand, a man is never forced to change his surname. His identity remains the same even after getting married to a woman. Sometimes a husband forces his wife to change the title of her name while in some circumstances women willingly change their title associating with her husband's title. Isn't it a sign of woman's identity of self-effacing? Women must consider that she herself has own identity to be recognised, why she should be recognised through her husband. Her identity should be individually separate.

In our country, a different set of codes is implemented socially for males and females. A female is inevitably marked with all the typical negative characteristics. A man is never expected to fall a drop of tears from his eyes even on someone's death otherwise it signifies below his dignity in the eyes of his concerning people. Only women are expected to cry over any event whether it is death or some other tragic events. On the other hand men are expected only to mourn over it without heaving sighs. When a boy cries for something, people, or many times women too comment derogatory remarks saying, he is crying like a girl, (*ladkiyo ki tarah rota hai*). A girl, according to the patriarchal system embodies weakness and a vulnerable heart. Sometimes, we hear from someone's tongue, if you can't do outside work why don't you wear bangles and sit inside the home. It is as if bangles signify weakness, and subverted position. Sometimes we come to know about the bizarre statements when people in our society associate men's activities with women's negative image, i.e. "you behave like a woman (*tum aurton jaise harkat karte ho*), you are talking like a woman (*tum to aurato jaisi baate kar rahe ho*), you are walking like a woman (*tum to aurton jaisi chal rahe ho).* These all stereotypical mentalities are imposed through patriarchal threads to constrain women. No one encourages a boy by giving the examples of some brave women's souls like Rani Laxmibai, and others. Even in most of rural societies, the game is divided on a gender basis. Parents never allow their girls to play kabaddi, cricket, or football, taking it categorically on a gender basis. So, it is the product of all patriarchal systems that obstruct girls from all round development. What they all do is only to associate women's characteristics with negativity. How can one divide certain activities on a gender basis? A girl's dressing sense, walking, way of talk, what to play, and what not, is all determined through the patriarchal world. She has to follow all such social codes but when a girl does not follow social codes, our society immediately categorises her character with some immoral or characterless images, i.e, she is a rogue girl or a girl of loose character.

Our Indian law is discriminatory where there is one rule for men and the other for women in some cases. Even after the passing of the law in 1919 'Cruelty against Women', the cruelties against women in their in-law's house persist today. No concrete action is taken into account. The whole constitutional order is monopolised as if it is a natural law. So, until our judicial law brings equal law practically, woman's suppression will go on. Dalit Women's equality is possible only when certain social structures and circumstances which hinder their free access to rights are modified in some appropriate way. Women's rights pertaining to equality are often devalued in the context of their feminine and sexual construction. The main problem is that the kinship structure in Indian society is built in such a discriminatory way that the choice of a woman in everything is determined by men thus binding women to men by excluding her democratic status. Public space has been structured in such a way that women remain always under surveillance where her every word is noticed by men. Sometimes it becomes risky for women to sustain political affairs when her unfit words lead her in losing her honour and that further brings the threat of physical harassment like rape. In some circumstances, a woman who is politically active and if her speech offend men, they target her and finding the opportunity never spare molesting and harassing her; sometimes victimized through rape. And so, in such cases, it is very difficult for a woman to continue her business in public affairs.

After examining so many factors the conclusion tells us that there are various forms which tend men to operate patriarchal oppression on women such as patriarchal oppression through cultural institutions e.g. religion, patriarchal power in the form of production, patriarchal power through sexual slavery, patriarchal power in paid work, patriarchal relations in the domestic works. Historical observations reveal that the main factors in women's marginalisation lie in educational deprivation, deprivation of women from political and religious knowledge, and the divining process of women. Sexual slavery is the crux of patriarchy; it is the key set of patriarchal practices. The main control over women by men takes place through sexuality, especially heterosexuality. It is the sexuality through which genders are constructed and identified socially. The elimination of patriarchy is not possible unless there is an elimination of sexual oppression. Although other patriarchal structures can be eliminated, it seems very difficult to eliminate sexual oppression since it functions from all modes and human beings cannot separate themselves without having sexual relations.

The other factor is land power which is bound with men. Although constitutionally women too have the right to have land from their father's land, practically the system is hardly into operation. Most of the families even today hardly provide land share to daughters. Women remain excluded from land power because men deny women to give land simply because she has to go to other's house, so why she should be given land who will later carry her land with herself. They also do say that a large amount of money is invested in a girl's marriage so it is equally compensation of land and marriage expense. Due to lack of property and land women most probably have to depend on their male members of the family. Man's class position is associated with production that is land while women's class position is tied through their sexual relationship with men because it is men who own land.

Sexual exploitation of women is the pitfall of their class exploitation because those who have land, power is all theirs and dominate those who don't possess the land. By the same token, the owners of production acquire the commodity of female sexual services, both from their own class as well as from the subordinate classes. So, the system of domination between man and woman will go on unless women are equally made owners of the land. Women should achieve more and more education so that they may have some knowledge to fight against their fundamental rights; to resist the domestic as well as perpetuating external violence, they should knit the network with other educated women to support the theory of feminism. According to Lerner, "a feminist world-view will enable women and men to free their mind from patriarchal thought and practice and at last to build a world free of dominance and hierarchy, a whole that is truly human" (Lerner 1986: 229). The myth that history has subordinated women, is rooted too much in the patriarchal mind of the people to come out from this interwoven concept. Now the time has arrived where women by breaking the old hierarchy are demanding their equal status and to be placed at the centre and to be talked in every event of the world. There is an urgent need of modification in the stereotypical behaviours of the patriarchal world.

Works Cited

Agarwal, Bina. *A Field of One's Own*. Cambridge: Cambridge Uni. Press, 1998. Print.

Aloysius, G. *Nationalism without a Nation in India*. New Delhi: Oxford University Press, 1997. Print.

Ambedkar, B.R. *Annihilation of Caste: The Annotated Critical Edition*. New Delhi: Nnavyana, 2014. Print.

Anand, Meena. *Dalit Women: Fear and Discrimination*. Delhi: Isha Books, 2005. Print

Anandi, S. J. Jeyaranajan and R. Krishnan. "Work, Caste and Competing Masculinities: Notes From a Tamil Village." *Economic and Political Weekly* 37.43 (n.d.): 4397-4406.

Angelou, Maya. *I Know Why the Caged Bird Sings*. New York: Ballantine Books, 2009. Print.

Bama. *Karukku*. 2nd ed. New Delhi: Oxford University Press, 2012. Print.

---. *Sangati*. Trans. Lakshmi Holstrom. New Delhi: Oxford University Press, 2005.

---. *Vanmam*. Trans. Malini Seshadri. New Delhi: Oxford Uni. Press, 2008. Print.

Basu, A. "Feminism Inverted: The Gendered Imagery and Rreal Women of Hindu Nationalism." *Women and the Hindu Right*. 1995. 158-180.

Beauvoir, Simon de. *The Second Sex*. London: David Campbell, 1970. Print.

Bennet, L. "Women, Poverty and Productivity in India." *Economic Development Institute Seminar* (1992): 43.

Berreman, G. "Sanskritisation as Female Oppression in India." Miller, D. *Sex and Gender Hierarchies*. Cambridge University Press, 1993. 366-392.

Beteille, A. *Inequality and Socila Change*. Delhi: Oxford University Press, 1972.

Bhattacharji, Sukumari. *Women and Society in Ancient India*. Calcutta: Basumati Corporation, 1994.

Bosrup, E. *Women's Role in Economic Development*. London: Allen and Unwin, 1970.

Brueck, Laura R. *Writing Resistance*. New York: Columbia Uni. Press, 2014. Press.

Butler, J. *Bodies That Matter*. New York, London: Routledge, 1993.

Butler, Judith. *Gendre Trouble*. 2nd ed. New York: Routledge, 1990. Print.

Caplan, P. *The Cultural Construction of Sexuality*. London: Routledge, 1987.

Chakravarti, Uma. "Conceptualising Brahmanical Patriarchy in Early India: Gender, Caste, Class and State." *Economic and Political Weekly* 28.14 (1993): 579-585.

---. "In Her Own Write: Writing from a Dalit Feminist Standpoint." *Indian*

International Centre Quarterly 39.3/4 (2012): 134-145. Web. 4 March 2017. <http://www.jstor.org/stable/24394281>.

Chakravorty, Gaytri Spivak. *Can the Subalterns Speak*. Chicago: Illinois, 1998. Print.

Chakravorty, Uma. *Gendering Caste Through a Feminist Lens*. Calcutta: Mandira Sen for STREE, 2013. Print.

Chalam, K.S. *Modernisation and Dalit Education: Ambedkar's Vision*. Jaipur: Rrawat Publications, 2008.

Chananna, K. "Socila Change or Socila Reform: Women, Education, and Family in Pre-Independence India." Mukhopadhyay, C and S. Seymour. *Women, Education and Family Structure in India*. Boulder, CO: Westview, 1994. 37-57.

Chandra, Sudhir. *Enslaved Daughters: Colonialism, Law and Women's Rights*. Delhi: Oxford University, 1998.

Chatterjee, Partha. "Colonialism, Nationalism, and Colonised Women: The Contest in India." *American Anthology* 16.04 (1989): 622-633. Web. 02 March 2017. <http:links.jstor.org?sisci>.

Chawdhry, P. *The Veiled Women: Shifting Gender Equations in Rural Haryana*. New Delhi: Oxford University Press, 1994.

Chodorow, Nancy. *The Reproduction of Mothering: Psychoanalysis and the Sociology of Gender*. Berkeley: Uni. of California Press, 1978. Print.

Cohn, Bernard. *An Anthropologist among Historians*. Delhi: Oxford University Press, 1987.

Collins, P.H. *Black Feminist Thought*. 2nd ed. New York: Routledge, 2000. Print.

---. *Black Sexual Politics*. New York: Routledge, 2004. Print.

Dangle, Arjun. *Poisoned Bread: Translations from Modern Marathi Dalit Literature*. Bombay: Orient Longman, 1992.

Das, S.K. "Narratives of Suffering: Caste and the Underprivileged." *Translating Caste*. Ed. Tapan Basu. Delhi: Katha, 2003.

Datar, Chahya. "Non-Brahmin Rendering of Feminism in Maharashtra: Is it a more Emancipatory Force?" *Economic and Political Weekly* 34.41 (1999): 2964-2968.

Davis, Angela Y. *Women, Race & Class*. New York: Vitage Books, 1981. Print.

Dhani, S.L. *Dr. B.R. Ambedkar: Man of Millennium for Social Justice*. Delhi: Kalpaz Publications, 2007.

Dube, Leela. *Women and Kinship: Comparative Perspectives on Gender in South and South-East Asia*. Delhi: Vistaar, 1997. Print.

Dworkin, A. *Right Wing Women: The Politics of Domesticated Women*. London: The Women's Press, 1983. Print.

Eisentein, Zillah R. *Capitalist Patriarchy and the Case for Socialist Feminism*. New York: Monthly Review Press, 1979. Print.

Engels, Friedrick. *The Origins of the Family, Private Property and the State*. Moscow: Progress Publishers, 1977. Print.

Fanon, Frantz. *Black Skin, White Masks.* Trans. Charles Lan Markmann. New York: Grove Press, 1952. Print.

---. *The Wretched of the Earth.* Trans. Constance Farrington. London: Penguin, 1963. Print.

Friedan, Betty. *The Feminist Mystique.* New York: Delhi Publishing Co, 1974. Print.

Fukazawa, H. *The Medieval Deccan.* Delhi: Oxford University Press, 1991.

Ganesh, Kamala. *Boundary Walls: Caste and Women in a Tamil Community.* Delhi: Hindustan Publishing Corporation, 1993.

Gangooli, Geetanjali. *Indian Feminisms: Law, Patriarchies and Violence in India.* U.S.A: Ashgate Publishing Ltd, 2007. Print.

Geeta, V and S.V.Rajadurai. *Towards a Non-Brahmin Millennium: From Iyothee Thass to Pariyar.* Kolkata: Samya, 1998.

Geeta, V. *Patriarchy.* 2nd ed. Kolkata: Mandira Sen for STREE, 2015. Print.

Ghosh, G.K and Shukla Gosh. *Dalit Women.* New Delhi: A.P.H Publishing Corporation, 1997.

Goody, J. *The Character of Kinship.* Cambridge: Cambridge University Press, 1973.

Gupta, C. *Sexuality, Obscenity, Community: Women, Muslim ansd the Hindu Public in Colonial India.* New York: Palgrave Macmillan, 2002.

Guru, Gopal & Surukkai. *The Cracked Mirror: An Indian Debate on Experience and Theory.* New Delhi: Oxford Uni. Press, 2012. Print.

Guru, Gopal. "Maharashtra's Women's Policy: Co-opting Feminism." *Economic and Political Weekly* 29.32 (1994): 2063-2065.

Habib, Irfan. *Essay in Indian History: Towards a Marxist Perception.* Delhi: Tulika, 1995.

Harishankar, Bharatiand and Ranjana Harish. Shakti: Multidisciplinary Perspective on Women's Empowerment in India. Jaipur: Rawat, 2003.

Heyer, J. "The Marginalisation of Dalits in a Modernising Economy." Harris-White, B. and J. Heyer. *The Comparative Political Economy of Development, Africa and South Asia.* London: Routledge, 2010. 225-247.

Hooks, Bell. *Ain't I A Woman: Black Women and Feminism.* New York: Routledge, 2015. Print.

---. *Feminist Theory: From Margins To Center.* New York: Routledge, 2015. Print.

Ilaiah, Kancha. *Buffalo Nationalism: A Critique of Spiritual Fascism.* Kolkata: Samya, 2004.

---. *Why I Am Not A Hindu.* Calcutta: Mandira Sen for Comment Samya, 2002. Print.

Irigaray, Luce. *An Ethics of Sexual Differences.* Trans. Carolyn Bruke and Gillian C. Gill. New York: Cornell University Press, 1993. Print.

Irigary, Luce. *This Sex Which Is Not One.* Trans. Catherine Porter with Carolyn Bruke. New York: Cornell Uni. Press, 1985. Print.

Jadhav, Narendra. *Ambedkar: Awakening India's Social Conscience.* New Delhi: Konark Publications Pvt. Ltd, 2014.

Jain, Jasbir. Women in Patriarchy: Cross Cultural Readings. Jaipur: Rawat Publications, 2005.

Jeffery, R. and A. Basu. *Girls Schooling Women's Autonomy and Fertility Change in South India.* Delhi: Sage, 1996.

Joshi, B. *Untouchable! The Voices of the Dalit Liberation Movement.* London: Zed Books, 1986.

Jr., Anthony J. Lemelle. *Black Masculinity and Sexual Politics.* New York: Routledge, 2010. Print.

Jung, Carl Gustav. *Aspects of the Feminine.* Trans. R.F.C. Hull. London, 2003.

Kamble, Baby. *The Prison we Broke.* Trans. Maya Pandit. New Delhi: Orient Blackswan, 2009. Print.

Kandasamy, Meena. "A Quest for Gender Equality in Meena Kandasamy's Touch." *International Journal on Studies in English and Literature* 02.05 (2014): 96-99. Web. 4 March 2016. <www.arcjournal.org>.

---. *The Gypsy Goddess: The Mighty Thunderclap of a Novel.* New Delhi: Fourth Eestate, 2014. Print.

---. *Touch.* Mumbai: Peacock Books, 2006.

Kannabiran, K. and V. Kannabiran. *De-Eroticising Assault: Essays on Modesty, Honour and Power.* Calcutta: Stree, 2002.

Kapdia, Karin. *Siva and Her Sisters.* Boulder: Westview Press, 1995.

Karve, I. *Kinship Organisation in India.* London: Asia Publishing House, 1953.

Kimmel, Michael S. *The Gendered Society.* 3rd ed. New York: Oxford Uni. Press, 2008. Print.

Kishwar, Madhu & Vanita, Ruth. *In Search of Answers: Women's Voices from Manushi.* 2nd ed. London: Zed Books, 1985. Print.

Kolenda, Pauline. *Regional Differences in Family Structures in India.* Jaipur: Rawat, 1987.

Kristeva, Julia. *Desire in Language: A Semiotic Approach to Literature and Art.* Basil Blackwell: Oxford, 1980. Print.

Lakshmanan, C. "Dalit Masculinities in Social Science Research: Revisiting a Tamil Village." *Economic and Political Weekly* 39.10 (2001): 4308-4311.

Lakshmi, Aishwarya. "The Liminal Body: The Language of Pain and Symbolism around Sati." *Feminst Review* 74 (2003): 81-97.

Lerner, Gerda. *The creation of Patriarchy.* New York: Oxford University Press, 1986. Print.

Leslie, Julia. *The Perfect Wife: The Orthodox Hindu Wife.* Delhi: Oxford University Press, 1989.

Limbale, Sharankumar. *The Outcaste.* Trans. Santosh Bhoomkar. New Delhi: Oxford University Press, 2003. Print.

---. *Towards an Aesthetic of Dalit Literature: History, Controversies and Considerations*. Trans. Alok Mukherjee. New Delhi: Orient Longman, 2004. Print.

Macwan, Joseph. *The Stepchild: Angaliyal.* New Delhi: Oxford University Press, 2004.

Mahananda, Saroj Kumar. *Dalit Literature & Historiography*. New Delhi: Pragati Publications, 2014. Print.

Maheshwari, Dr. V.K. "Macaulay's Minute On Indian Education." 7 July 2012. Web. 9 March 2017. <ww.vkmaheshwari.com>.

Malik, Bela. "Untouchability and Dalit Women's Oppression." *Economic and Political Weekly* 34.16 (1999): 323-324.

Massey, James. *Downtrodden: The Struggle of India's Dalits For Identity, Soliderity and Liberation*. Geneva: WCC Publishers, 1997.

---. *Indigenous People: Dalits: Dalit Issues in Today's Theological Debate*. Delhi: ISPCK, 1994.

Menon, Nivedita. *Seeing Like A Feminist.* New Delhi: Penguin Books, 2012. Print.

Millet, Kate. *Sexual Politics*. New York: University of Illiniois Press, 1970. Print.

Mistry, Cyrus. *The Chronicle of a Corpse Bearer.* New Delhi: Aleph, 2012. Print.

Mitchel, Juliet. *Women's Estate*. London: Penguin, 1971. Print.

Mohanty, Manoranjan. *Class, Caste, Gender: Readings In Indian Government And Politics.* New Delhi: Sage Publications Pvt. Ltd, 2008.

Moi, Toril. *Sexual/Textual Politics: Feminist Literary Theory*. New York: Routledge, 1988. Print.

Moon, Meenakshi and Urmila Pawar. *We Also Made History: Women in the Ambedkar Movement*. New Delhi: Zubaan, 2008.

Mukherjee, Meenakshi. "Rreview: Women Writing." *Economic and Political Weekly* 38.27 (2003): 2837-2839.

Narayan, Badri. *Women Heroes and Dalit Aassertion in North India*. New Delhi: Sage Publications India Pvt Ltd, 2006. Print.

Neetha, N. and I. Mazundar. "Gender Dimensions: Employment Trends in India." *Economic and Political Weekly* 46.43 (2011): 118-126.

Nnaemeka, Obioma, ed. *The Politics of (M)Othering*. London: Routledge, 1997. Print.

Nongbri, T. "Gender and the Khasi Family Structures." Uberio, P. *Family, Kinship and Marraige in India*. Delhi: Oxford University Press, 1993.

Okeke, Phil E. "Reconfiguring Tradition: Women's Rights and Social Status in Contemporary Nigeria." *African Today* 47.01 (2000): 49-63. Web. 17 Octeober 2016. <http://www.jstor.org/stable/4187307>.

P.H.Collins. *Black Sexual Politics: African Americans, Gender, And The New Racism.* New York: Routledge, 2004. Print.

Pal, R.M. and G.S. Bhargava. *Human Rights of Dalits: Societal Violation*. New Delhi: Gyan Publishing House, 2001.

Pawar, Urmila. *The Wave of My Life: A Dalit Woman's Memoir.* New Delhi: Popular Prakashan, 2008. Print.

Podder, Bhagirath. *The Untouchables in India.* New Delhi: Sarup and Sons, 2001.

Ponnacha, Veena. "Challenging Caste and Gender Ideologies." *Economic and Political Weekly* 28.48 (2003): 5047-5049.

Prasad, Amar Nath and M.G. Gaijan. *Dalit Literature: A Critical Exploration.* New Delhi, 2007.

Price, P. *Kingship and Political Practices in Colonial India.* Cambridge: Cambridge University Press, 1996.

Rajan, R. Sundar. *Real and Imagined Women: Gender, Culture and Postcolonialism.* London: Routledge, 1993.

Rajan, Rajeswari Sundar. "Is the Hindu Goddess a Feminist?" *Economic and Political Weekly* 33.44 (1998): 34-38.

Rao, Anupama. *Gender & Caste.* New Delhi: Kali for Women, 2003. Print.

---. "Sexuality and the Family Form." *Economic and Political Weekly* 40.08 (2005): 715-718. Web. 03 March 2016. <http://www.jstor.org/stable/4416226>.

Rao, Yagato Chinna. *Writing Dalit History and Other Essays.* New Delhi: Kanishka Publishers, 2007.

Rege, S. "Caste and Gender: The Violence againsr Dalit Women in India." Jogdand, P. G. *Dalit Women in India: Issues and Perspectives.* New Delhi: Gyan Publishing House, 1995. 18-36.

Rege, Sharmila. "Dalit Women Talk Differently: A Critique of 'Difference' and Towards a Dalit Feminist Standpoint." *Economic and Political Weekly* 33.44 (1998): 39-46. Web. 08 March 2016. <http://www.jstor.org/stable/4407323>.

---. "'Real Feminism' and Dalit Women: Scripts of Denial and Accusation." *Economic and Political Weekly* 35.06 (2000): 492-495.

---. *Writing Caste Writing Gender: Narrating Dalit Women's Testimonies.* New Delhi: Zubaan, 2006. Print.

Roussaeu, Jean Jacques. *The Social Contract or Principles of Political Rights.* New Delhi: E.P. Dutton & Co, 1913. Print.

Said, Edward. *Orientalism: The Concept of Orient.* New York: Routledge & Kegan Paul Ltd, 1978. Print.

Sangari, K. and S.Vaid. *Recasting Women: Essay in Colonial History.* New Delhi: Kali for Women, 1989.

Sangari, Kumkum. "Politics of Diversity: Religious Communities and Multiple Patriarchies." *Economic and Political Weekly* 30.52 (1995): 3381-3389. Web. 01 11 2016. <www.jstor.org/stable/4403624>.

Sarukkai, S. "Dalit Experience and Theory." *Economic and Political Weekly* 42.40 (2007): 4043-4048.

Sen, Amartya. *Social Exclusion: Concept, Application, Scrutiny.* New Delhi: Critical Quest, 2004.

Sharma, R.P. *Woman in Hindu Literature.* New Delhi: Gyan Publishing House, 1995.

Sharma, R.S. *Material Culture and Social Formations.* Delhi: Macmillan, 1983.

Shinde, Tarabai. *Stri Purusha Tulana.* Madras: Oxford Uni. Press, 1994. Print.

Shirman, R. "World of Dalit Women." *Economic and Political Weekly* 39.50 (2004): 5305-5306.

Shivkumar, Vaishali. "A Dalit Woman Under a Strong Clutch of Patriarchy: A Comprehensive Study of The Grip of Change." *Language In India* 13.04 (2013): 1930-2940. Web. 03 March 2016. <www.languageinindia.com>.

Showalter, Elaine, ed. *The New Feminist Criticism.* New York: Pantheon Books, 1985. Print.

Shriman, Rachel. "Review: World of Dalit Women." *Economic and Political Weekly* 39.50 (2004): 5305-5306.

Sinde, Tarabai. *Stri Purusha Tulana.* Trans. Rosalind O'Hanlon. Madras: Oxford University Place, 1994.

Singh, Chandra Nisha. *Only So Far and No Further: Radical Feminism and Women's Writing.* New Delhi: Atlanta Publishers and Distributors, 2007. Print.

Singh, Ekta. *Caste System in India: A Historical Perspective.* Delhi: Kalpaz Publication, 2004.

Singh, Karan. *Dalitism and Feminism.* New Delhi: Creative Books, 2011. Print.

Singh, Smriti. "Narrating Subaltern Consciousness: Bama's Sangati." *International Journal of English and Literature* 5.5 (2014): 113-118. Web. 4 November 2016. <http:www.academicjournals.org/IJEL>.

Sircar, Roopali. *The Twice Colonised Women: Women in African Literature.* New Delhi: Creative Books, 1995. Print.

Sreenvias, Mytheli. "Conjugality and Capital: Gender, Families, and Property under Colonial Law in India." *Journal of Asian Studies* 04 (2004): 63.

Srinivas, M.N. *Social Change in Modern India.* Bombay: Oxford University Press, 1972.

Still, Clarinda. *Dalit Women: Honour and Patriarchy in South India.* New Delhi: Social Science Press, 2014. Print.

Strauss, Claude Levi. *The Element Structures of Kinship.* Boston: Beacon Press, 1949. Print.

Sumanakshar, S.P. *Buddha to Ambedkar.* Delhi: Bhartiya Dalit Sahitya, 2002.

Tagore, Rabindra Nath. *The Home and the World.* Trans. Surendra Nath Tagore. New York: Macmillan, 1915. Print.

Teltumbde, Anand. *The Persistence of Caste.* New Delhi: Navyana, 2010. Print.

Thappar, Romila. *From Lineage to State.* Delhi: Oxford University Press, 1984.

Tharu, Susie and Tejaswini Niranjana. "Problems for a Contemporary Theory of Gender." *Social Scientist* 22.03 (1994): 93-117.

Tharu, Susie. "The Impossible Subject: Caste and the Gendered Body." *Economic and Political Weekly* 31.22 (1996): 1311-1315.

"The Diffference – Deferral of a Colonial Modernity." *Tensions of Empire.* Ed. Fredrick Cooper & Ann Laura Stoler. London & England: University of California, 1997. 346-373. Print.

Uberio, P. *Family, Kinship and Marriage in India.* Delhi: Oxford University Press, 1993.

Valmiki, Omparkash. *Joothan: A Dalit's Life.* Trans. Arun Prabha Mukherjee. Kolkata: Samya, 2003. Print.

Visweswaran, Kamala. *Fictions of Feminist Ethnography.* Minneapolis: University of Minnesota, 1995. Print.

Walbi, Sylvia. "Theorising Patriarchy." *Sociology* 23.02 (1989): 213-234. Web. 01 November 2016. <http://www.jstor.org/stable/42853921>.

walker, Alice. *In search Of Our Moher's Garden.* New York: Hartcourt Brace Johonovich, 1983. Print.

Walker, Alice. *The Colour Purple.* London: Phoenix, 2004. Print.

Watkins, Gloria. *Ain't I A Woman: Black Women and Feminism.* Boston: Ma South End Press, 1981. Print.

Yadav, Mamta. *Dalits in India: Past and Present.* New Delhi: Omega Publications, 2010. print.

Zelliot, Eleanor. *Faces of Feminine, Ancient, Medieval, Modern.* Ed. Mandakranta Bose. Delhi: Oxford University Press, 2000.

---. *From Untouchables to Dalit: Essays on the Ambedkar Movement.* New Delhi: Manohar Publications, 1992.

Index